DECORATIVE FLOORS OF
VENICE

DECORATIVE FLOORS OF

VENICE

TUDY SAMMARTINI

PHOTOGRAPHY BY GABRIELE CROZZOLI

FOREWORD BY JOHN JULIUS NORWICH

MERRELL

FOREWORD *by John Julius Norwich*

This is, to my knowledge, the first book that has ever been written about the floors of Venice. Is there, one wonders, any other city about whose floors a book *could* be written? *The Floors of London*, even *The Floors of Paris*, would be dull publications indeed. But Venice is an exception to every rule. She is the one city in the world who has made her floors of stone, marble and mosaic – as she has made so much else – into an art form, and this ravishing book stands witness to her achievement.

Why did these Venetians choose these materials in the first place? For one thing, Venice in the high summer can be extremely hot, and they knew that floors of stone and marble were cooler than any others. A good parquet might admittedly have been more practical in winter, when the cold can be perishing: but they were, after all, hugely successful merchants and traders, whose city marked the crossroads between the East and West. Not only were they rich enough to import as much glorious polychrome marble as they needed; they could also afford thick carpets that kept their feet warm during the winter months. Moreover, stone and marble keep out the damp; wood does not.

The decorative tradition started early: for proof of that we have only to look at the floors of the cathedral in Torcello, of San Donato in Murano and above all of St Mark's itself. But why – the question cannot be avoided – did those early Venetians, unlike any of their contemporaries, pay every bit as much attention to what lay under their feet as to what rose over their heads? Would it be to fanciful to suggest that it might have been partly because, in a city built on water, the endlessly shimmering reflections of their churches and palaces constantly attracted their gaze downward? If so, they would have quickly grown to expect as much colour, as much play of light and of movement, below their line of sight as above it. Besides, the art of what Ruskin called incrustation – the inlaying into stone or marble walls of slabs of porphyry, verd-antique and other materials – was a traditional feature of Venetian architecture, particularly in Byzantine days and then again during the Early Renaissance in the late fifteenth century: the church of the Miracoli, the Scuola Grande di San Marco and Palazzo Dario are cases in point. If even walls could be inlaid, why not floors too?

Venice is, *par excellence*, a city of detail. Here more than anywhere else we have to keep our eyes roving – from side to side, but even more importantly up and down – if we are not to miss the little touches of imagination and fantasy that surround us wherever we go. Yet even then, however well we may think we know the city, there will always be new discoveries to surprise and enchant us. Of such discoveries this book is a treasure-house, and I am more than grateful to its author and its superb photographer: they have taught me much.

To Paolo

First published in English in 2000 by
Merrell Publishers Limited
42 Southwark Street, London SE1 1UN
www.merrellpublishers.com

English language edition © Merrell Publishers Limited

First published 1999 by Vianello Libri
Copyright © 1999 Edizione Grafiche Vianello srl/Vianello Libri

Distributed in the USA and Canada by Rizzoli International Publications, Inc.
through St Martin's Press, 175 Fifth Avenue, New York, New York 10010

British Library Cataloguing-in-Publication Data
Sammartini, Tudy
Decorative floors of Venice
1.Floors – Italy – Venice 2.Flooring, Tile 3.Tiles in interior decoration – Italy – Venice
4.Pavements, Mosaic – Italy – Venice
I.Title II.Crozzoli, Gabriele
747.4'094531

ISBN 1 85894 108 3

Designed by Scibilia & Scibilia
Jacket designed by Matthew Hervey
Text layout by Karen Wilks

English translation by Giles Watson
Edited by Julian Honer

Printed and bound in Italy

Jacket:
Monastery of San Domenico, detail of Grand Staircase inlaid marble floor (1666) attributed to
Baldassare Longhena and completed by Antonio Bonini (for details, see pp. 87 and 184)

CONTENTS

INTRODUCTION *by Elena Bassi*

In Venice, distances are short. It takes only an hour or so to walk from one end of the city to the other. The townscape is made up of a cluster of islets, each of which forms a miniature 'town centre' with its own church, campanile (or bell-tower), a square (known as a campo) and shops nestling in among the houses. Most of the residential buildings have several entrances, for it is a uniquely Venetian tradition that each apartment should be independent, with its own door and entrance hall. Whether large or small, the houses in Venice are laid out to a very similar plan and rendered more attractive to live in by various forms of decoration.

Flooring is very much part of such ornamentation. The bright colours and rich, artistic designs of Venice's floors suggest exotic carpets, scattered to beautify the rooms of the city's palazzi.

Floors in Venetian mosaic, also known as terrazzo, have since time immemorial enabled *terrazeri* artists to give free rein to their imagination in accordance with the styles of the various periods, all of which are carefully documented in this lavishly illustrated volume. For this book presents a wide range of floor types, dating from as long ago as the ninth century through to present-day examples, often part-restored and part-conserved in historic buildings with a glorious past.

Nevertheless, floors do more than just bear living testimony to the changing tastes of their owners. They also provide us with a sort of concentrated history of art that passes from the minute detail of ancient *opus tessellatum* to the broad fascias and generously proportioned panels of the sixteenth-, seventeenth- and eighteenth-century geometrical compositions adorning the buildings designed by such architects as Andrea Palladio, Baldassare Longhena, Antonio Gaspari and Giorgio Massari.

This book, the first complete, in-depth investigation of the subject, examines a large number of significant examples that are characteristic of the techniques, symbolism and tastes of each period, from the earliest mosaics of the Byzantine and Ravenna schools to floors that were completed only recently. There emerges evidence of an intriguing relationship between the decoration of ceilings and the figurative designs on the floors, both of which are strongly influenced by the architectural structure of the buildings in which they are located.

Although there are no limits to the creativity of individual artists in inventing ever-new decorative motifs or selecting and matching the variously coloured stone and marble tesserae, Venetian *terrazeri* have always had as their benchmark the incomparable *opus tessellatum* of the flooring in St Mark's Basilica, which is an inexhaustible source of inspiration for all the 'carpets' that grace the city's interiors.

pages 8–9
Piazza San Marco today: the level was raised by about one metre and the square paved with slabs of Euganean trachyte and bands of Istrian stone in 1723, to a design by Andrea Tirali.

page 10
The warm glow of the sunset transforms the waters of the canal into a glittering floor.

11

COLOURS AND SYMBOLS IN VENETIAN FLOORS

These are Dante's words when, on entering the first ring of Purgatory, he finds himself contemplating a marvellous spectacle. The walls and floors are carved with talking figures. The proud, punished by having to carry a rock on their shoulders, are forced to bend over as they walk and gain redemption by listening to what the figures say.

Today, haste-induced pride keeps our gaze fixed at eye-level. It seems we are able to see only what lies in front of our noses. No one allows history-rich ceilings and floors to speak. And yet how much they would still have to tell us if only we were to pause and take the time to listen.

It has not always been like this. Let us pretend for a moment that we are in Venice some time between the ninth and thirteenth centuries. The whole city is a riot of colour. And yet the only surviving record of that splendour is to be found in the city's floors.

"At Murano, every fragment is itself variegated, and all are arranged with a skill and feeling not to be taught, and to be observed with great reverence." These are the words with which Ruskin describes the mosaic floor of the church of Santi Maria e Donato. He notes that the church is not just one of the most precious monuments in Italy, but also one whose floor shows "the beginning of that mighty spirit of Venetian colour, which was to be consummated in Titian".

Let us take a few steps further back in time. In early Christian churches, the floor was decorated with a single continuous band that formed a geometrical network of straight lines and curves. The grid itself could constitute the pattern or it might be filled with coloured patterns. The uninterrupted line along which it was traced symbolized eternity.

In the mosaic fragments of the ninth-century Benedictine church of Sant'Ilario, the band forms a series of circles, some of which are decorated with stylized representations of animals and flowers, recurrent motifs in the late classical floors of both the Western and Eastern Roman Empires. The patterns, in black and white with occasional traces of red, are linear and elementary (*opus alexandrinum*), and to interpret them one only has to glance at the history of the period. In the ninth century the lagoon came under the influence of the Carolingians, who dominated much of the Italian peninsula, particularly in the north. The markedly geometrical pattern of the floor at Sant'Ilario echoes the cloths of Charlemagne. Nonetheless, the Roman tradition, of which Aquileia is a fine example, continued. The material used was always recycled and of ancient origin, in an attempt to maintain a functional link with the past. In the case of Venice, this meant Rome, for it should not be forgotten that the lagoon city was founded by refugees fleeing from Roman *castra* that were under threat from barbarian invasions.

In the floor of the Benedictine church of San Nicolò di Lido, dating from the mid-eleventh century, the grid and floral elements intertwine to form an

Our feet had not yet walked up there,
when I became aware that the bank around
was less steep,
and of snow-white marble adorned with such
carvings as would put Polycletus,
or even Nature herself, to shame.
(Dante, 'Purgatory', Canto X, vv. 28–33)

page 12
Fondazione Querini Stampalia: Carlo Scarpa connected the ground floor to the canal along asymmetrically arranged flights of steps.

Church of San Nicolò di Lido, floor, mid-eleventh century.

impressive arabesque of great artistry that bears witness to its late classical inspiration. The surviving fragments of the floor in San Lorenzo were probably designed in the same tradition.

However, Venice, a city that rose up from the sea, was the daughter of Rome in two senses, thanks to its links with Byzantium, capital of the Roman Empire in the East. We could mention, for example, Narses, who in the sixth century founded at Venice the twin churches of San Giminiano and San Teodoro, on the site where St Mark's Basilica was later to be built. The similarities and ties between the two shores of the Adriatic are easy to comprehend, for it is as if the sea functioned more as a bridge than a barrier. The earliest churches therefore reveal the exquisite chromatic effects of Byzantium in luminous fragments that symbolize the divine *claritas* of the Celestial Jerusalem. In contrast, their exteriors create effects of light and shade, setting volumes against spaces and exploiting the complementary colours of warm pink brick and white marble in a perfect Venetian-Byzantine style. It was at this time that master mosaicists were decorating places of worship with mosaic floors, transforming porphyry, terracotta and stone into brightly coloured tesserae that were assembled to make elaborate geometrical patterns, floral motifs and mythological animals. Elements from the Roman, pagan, Christian, Byzantine and Arab worlds were blended together. The most marked of these influences came from Byzantium, as a result of the diaspora of monks and mosaicists that followed the iconoclast persecutions proclaimed in 726 by Emperor Leo III. Little is known of these artisans but we may assume that they operated in teams that moved from one site to another. Consequently, some floors have a single overall design while others present discrepancies resulting from suspensions and resumptions of work or from unorthodox restoration.

One example of such mixing of styles can be seen in the church of San Zaccaria, where the natural treatment of animal figures is reminiscent both of the fourth-century mosaic floors at Aquileia and of those at Skhira in Tunisia. In contrast, the marble slabs in San Donato, which are Roman gravestones turned back to front, bear witness to a continuity of tradition. In the twelfth century there is a marked trend towards a greater use of colour, perhaps because of the arrival of large numbers of artisans from the East.

Torcello, however, is an unusual case. The floor of the lower basilica, the most ancient of those still in their original location, is contemporary with that in Sant'Ilario and, as far as can be deduced from the visible fragments, is in the late classical style of all mosaic (*opus tessellatum*). In contrast, the floor in the upper part reflects the Byzantine and Romanesque tastes for cut pieces (*opus sectile*), a procedure that was adopted only for wealthier churches. The complete absence of figures is remarkable, and is possibly owing to a subsequent intervention inspired by iconoclasm. The unique nature and innovative execution – it was undoubtedly completed over a short period of time to a very precise plan – as well as its allusions to the figures in the presbytery make it likely that it was executed later than the interiors of St Mark's or San Donato.

There are examples of the decorative motifs seen in Venice's medieval floors not just at Aquileia and Rome but even in what is now Tunisia, such as the triangular pattern of the floor from a villa near the rich, olive oil-producing centre of Thysdrus. The mosaic, which dates from the second or third century AD, is currently conserved in the museum at El Djem. There was a feeling that, in effect, the Mediterranean was just a large lake. Any part of it could be reached by ship.

Let us pretend that we have the task assigned to the architect monk who designed St Mark's Basilica. As he drew up the plan for the floor, he genuinely believed he was bringing heaven and earth together. That was why he used shapes not only from traditional heritage but also ones that evoke and give voice to figures from Christian mysticism. In the plan of St Mark's, the four arms of a Greek cross intersect in a square in which a circle represents a projection of the dome of the Ascension. This point is the fulcrum of the entire edifice. The correspondence between summit and base represents the meeting of heaven and earth. In mystical symbolism, the circle is the development of the centre, representing its dynamic aspect, and the square is its static manifestation. The circle symbolizes heaven, while the square is the earth and therefore paradise on earth. Another emblematic motif is the dodecagon, which we find in the entrance of the Porta di San Pietro and at the start of the presbytery. Euclid and Plato held it to be the perfect shape; for Luca Pacioli, whose treatise *De Divina Proportione* so influenced learning in Venice, it represented 'divinity' in mathematics, while in Christian thought the dodecagon symbolized the twelve tribes of Israel and the twelve prophecies in the Book of Revelation.

But the most surprising aspect is the harmonious, unified conception of all the different parts of the church. In particular, there is a perfect iconographic correspondence between the mosaics in the vaults and the geometric patterns of the floor. The symbols below tell the same story as the figures overhead to form a reverse cosmogony in which the heavens are

Basilica of Santa Maria Assunta at Torcello, lower floor, ninth century.

COLOURS AND SYMBOLS IN VENETIAN FLOORS

reflected. The key to these images has been lost with the passage of time. The symbols themselves have acquired new meanings and some have even been replaced by other figures. Nevertheless, many of the representations of animals can be explained by referring to medieval bestiaries, which provided a Christian interpretation of pagan mythology. Some of the more frequent animal images include: the eagle, the queen of the skies which was reputed to be able to acquire wisdom by looking straight into the sun; the lion, king of the desert, which embodied majesty, courage and justice, and was even, on occasion, a *figura Christi,* or representation of Christ; and the peacock, which symbolized the Resurrection and immortality. There are also deer, emblematic of faith in God, and mythological monsters, such as griffins and basilisks, representing evil.

The floor of St Mark's, the symbol of Venice and, like the Serene Republic herself, in constant evolution, is the lodestar and inspiration for all the other floors in the city.

We move now into a Gothic atmosphere. It is as if the Venetians wanted to surround themselves with a new range of colours that spilled out of the buildings on to the outside walls, to be reflected in the waters of the canals and lagoon in a dazzling kaleidoscope of ever-changing light.

Pilgrims who passed through on their way to the Holy Land were astonished at the sight of the Grand Canal and the frescoed palazzi that were mirrored in its surface. One of the most ancient examples can be seen at the Museo Correr, where there are two fragments from the façade of a house at San Giuliano, near St Mark's, which feature allegorical representations of the four theological virtues nestling in floral Gothic niches. In addition, the grey Venice left behind by the passage of time has miraculously preserved the figures over the loggia in the garden of Palazzo Contarini Corfu. Ca' d'Oro, so called because of the brilliant splendour of its decorations by Zuane de Franza (Jean Charlier), is a superb example of this triumph of colour. It was executed in 1431. Thereafter, the city was to be transformed by colour. This can be seen from the *teleri,* the vast cyclical narrative paintings by Venetian artists dating from the late fifteenth century, such as the *Miracle of the Relic of the True Cross* by Carpaccio, and even more clearly in the *Procession of the Cross in the Piazza San Marco* by Gentile Bellini, from 1496, which highlights the ancient paving in the square, laid in 1264. The herring-bone-patterned terracotta surface is enhanced by longitudinal bands of Istrian stone that draw attention to the focal point of the church itself. This design was crucial in, among other things, compensating for the eccentric shape of the square. Its appearance today is that left after the intervention of Andrea Tirali, who raised the level by one metre in 1723. The brick was replaced by trachyte slabs decorated only by two parallel strips in Istrian stone so that the campanile, or bell-tower, which is still in terracotta brick, looks as if it no

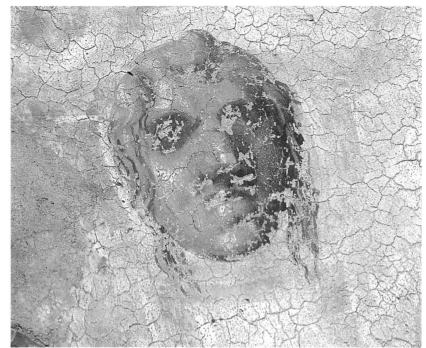

longer fits in with its surroundings. On the subject of outdoor pavings in general, Marc'Antonio Sabellico, in his work *Del sito di Venezia città* of 1502, relates that the public streets "are paved in brick". Over the years, the bricks were replaced by slabs of trachyte, known as *salizade*. We can see them in

Gentile Bellini, *Procession of the Cross in the Piazza San Marco*, 1496, Gallerie dell'Accademia.

Canaletto's *Perspective, Courtyard and Portico of a Building*, painted in 1765, which earned the artist admission to the Accademia. Today, we can reconstruct the original appearance of the square by looking at the sacristy of the church of Madonna dell'Orto in Cannaregio, which has remained as it was in the fourteenth century.

Now we move on to the Renaissance and with it that triumph of colour that found its most glorious expression in the church of Santa Maria dei Miracoli (1481–94). A place of popular devotion, it is a marble-clad and floored 'casket', built to house a miracle-working image of the Virgin Mary. The church itself is dedicated to the Immaculate Conception, a dogma only ratified in 1854 and which it anticipated by nearly four centuries. Architecturally, the building is extremely interesting. There is a Tuscan feel to the pillars on the outside (the Amadi family, who sponsored the project, were merchants from Tuscany), while the vaults of the ceiling are reminiscent of Alberti. But, as always in Venice, the marks of the past are well in evidence. Its perfect, self-contained lines recall those of late classical sarcophagi, and indeed the Venetians of the day considered it second only to St Mark's in beauty.

At almost exactly the same time, the walls of St Mark's were clad in precious marble, and after the fall of Constantinople to the Turks in 1453, Venice, the daughter of Byzantium, witnessed a sudden surge in the popularity of domed Greek cross-plan churches built in the characteristic aesthetic of the Renaissance style.

Other floors that are no longer extant, such as the one in the church of San Giovanni Evangelista, were relaid in precious materials in the same way as that of Santa Maria dei Miracoli. It should be borne in mind, however, that these were exceptions to the general rule of the time, which dictated, as Sabellico notes, floors in a red and white chequered pattern.

Historical records make little mention of floors, but one exception is the writing of Francesco Sansovino, who in 1580 described Santa Maria dei Miracoli, noting that its coloured cladding had the sumptuous appearance of "the finest marble, and inside was the same, both on the floor and all over". Even more explicit are the words of Leon Battista Alberti, who, in his *De re aedificatoria* written in the mid-fifteenth century, went so far as to demand that floors should be orchestrated like a symphony. He recommended that "the whole floor should be covered with musical and geometrical lines and shapes so that the attention of observers would be by all means drawn to the arts" – excellent advice for Venice, a city in which every church is also a concert hall.

As the Renaissance reached its height, the ceaseless study of architectural proportions meant that, where truly sensitive artists were at work, buildings would be constructed with a precise relationship between the constituent parts.

Out of doors, flooring had the practical function of identifying a space and of delimiting through its decoration the various qualities or sacred nature of a church courtyard, and to this was now added the role of projecting the façade on to the ground. The system can still be clearly seen in Andrea Palladio's church of the Redentore, where the three elements of the external courtyard, façade and internal floor complement each other. This is not all, for the pattern of colours in the presbytery forms a plan drawing of the apses and dome, and the three steps clearly separate this special place from the nave, which is decorated in the usual red and white squares. Palladio also designed the front courtyard of the monastery of the Carità, completed between 1568 and 1571, and illustrated in a nineteenth-century watercolour conserved in the library of the Accademia. The room alternates the light shades of the walls with the pink of the columns and the Doric frieze, which are mirrored in the projection on the flooring.

It was nearly always the case that the architect who made the plans for the building also designed the floor. Unfortunately, with few exceptions (among

Villa near Thysdrus (Tunisia), floor from the second to third centuries ad, El Djem museum (from Georges Tradier, *Mosaïques Romaines de Tunisie*, Tunis, Cérès Productions, 1986).

which are the sketches by Baldassare Longhena for the central rose window and presbytery of the church of Santa Maria della Salute), no floor designs have come down to us. It is probably to Longhena again, although there is no certain proof, that we owe the earliest example of a Florentine-style floor, laid in 1666 on the landings of the main staircase at the monastery of San Domenico. By now, we have arrived at the height of the Baroque period.

Many of the Baroque floors can be attributed to a specific artist. For example, the landings at Ca' Zenobio are by Antonio Gaspari, the architect who completed many of the buildings left unfinished by his master, Longhena. Gaspari was also responsible for the landings and entrance hall at Ca' Pesaro, one of the few examples of labyrinthine design.

Some of the other major artists active in the eighteenth century include Domenico Rossi, who was at work in the church of the Gesuiti, replacing the traditional red and white chequered pattern with a design based on a divided double Greek cross, which started a new fashion. Andrea Tirali was at San Nicolò da Tolentino, Giorgio Massari at San Marcuola, and his pupil Bernardino Maccaruzzi worked on the Casino Venier and the Scuola della Carità, today galleries of the Accademia.

Terrazzo flooring, also known as Venetian mosaic, is particularly interesting. Made from marble tesserae laid in stucco and lime, terrazzo's elasticity and light weight render it ideal for the structure of buildings in Venice. The *terrazeri*, as terrazzo mosaicists were called, were regarded as true artists and have jealously handed the secrets of their craft down from father to son right to the present day. Traditional terrazzo took the form of a uniform covering of coloured stones without a precise pattern. There are very few examples of other terrazzo floors before the end of the seventeenth century, when the 'Sansovino-style' beams of the city's halls began to be covered up by stuccoed and frescoed ceilings. The artists responsible frequently conceived a global design, as can be seen at Palazzo Barbarigo and Palazzo Pisani Moretta. The eighteenth century is generally considered to be Venice's *siècle d'or*. Noblewomen and their gallants strolled as if to the strains of a Vivaldi violin sonata under the watchful eye of their low-born counterparts, who chatted in the campielli while haughty powder-daubed aristocrats donned the traditional bauta, or mask, as they hurried off on 'secret missions'. Since the sixteenth century, the casini, or private clubs, of Venice had been places for amorous encounters, good conversation and

Antonio Canal, known as Canaletto, *Perspective, Courtyard and Portico of a Building*, 1765, Gallerie dell'Accademia.

Convento della Carità,
nineteenth-century floor
design of The Tablino,
today the library of
the Accademia (from
Elena Bassi, *Il Convento
della Carità*, Venice,
Centro Internazionale di
Studi di Architettura
A. Palladio, 1971).

gaming, as well as the meeting places of the free spirits who were open to the new ideas arriving from across the Alps. By the eighteenth century, casini were renowned not only for the high social standing of their owners and their guests but also for the elegance of their interiors, which were masterpieces of 'the architecture of discretion'. Entry was gained by making one's way along apparently anonymous corridors, up narrow stairs and through secret passages, where peep-holes, some in the floor, enabled one to check who was arriving. At the end of the route lay elegantly decorated rooms with frescoed ceilings, stuccoed walls and mirrors, where latticework partitions enabled patrons to listen unseen to the musicians. The floors were an integral part of the overall design, as is clear from the so-called Casin del Baffo, where the unusual geometrical pattern of the flooring suggests that it might have been used for gaming.

The city was one vast, brightly painted stage. In campo Santo Stefano there were still clear traces of the lively scene of more than a century earlier, as Moschini reports. Three of the houses had frescoes by Giorgione, one was frescoed by Tintoretto, Palazzo Loredan had frescoes by Salviati, those on Palazzo Barbaro were by Sante Zago, and Palazzo Morosini's were by Antonio Vassilacchi, known as l'Aliense.

As the commemoration of historical events became less important, giving way to decoration, Venice's links with the East shifted from representation to mere allusion. The symbolic function of art, in line with the new French theories, lost its concrete significance and acquired an aesthetic meaning. One example of this is the floor of Palazzo Trevisan Moro, where exotic animals stalk islands dotted with pagodas and palm-trees. In Palazzo Condulmer, in contrast, the family crest depicted on the floor is transformed into a large jewel in precious materials such as agate and breccia marble from the East.

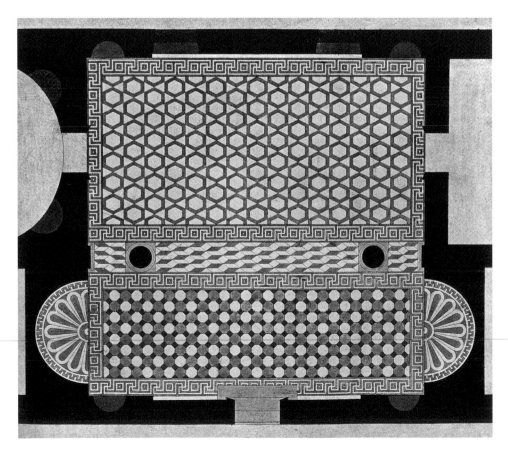

In fact, it was customary in noble houses to feature the family crest in the decoration on the floor. On occasion, this led to fierce rivalry as aristocrats vied with each other to produce the most ostentatious design. The winners were probably the

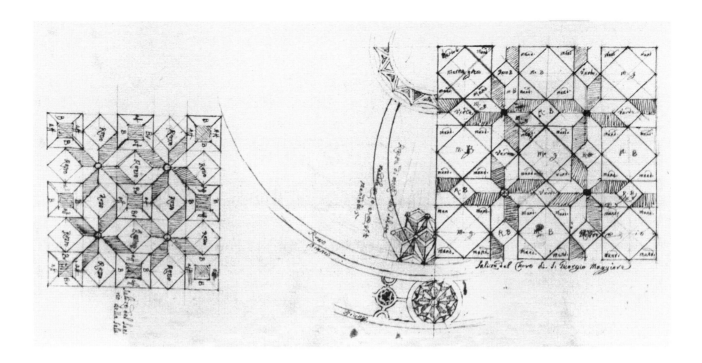

powerful Mocenigo family, whose six-square-metre crest was studded with lapis lazuli and gold tesserae. In contrast, the Piovene floor is remarkable for another reason. It features a late classical terrazzo design from the island of Cyprus, in memory of Guido Piovene, who died heroically during the siege of Nicosia.

The tradition continued, in almost tongue-in-cheek fashion, into the nineteenth century. Flamboyance was the order of the day, but at the height of this revival, the meaning of the language was lost. Naturally, as content declined, form took over. Palazzo Cavalli Franchetti was labelled neo-Gothic and the Banca Commerciale Italiana building was classed as neo-Renaissance, but the two styles look as if they have no deeper significance. Great technical precision was, however, brought into play by such masters as Michelangelo Guggenheim, Carlo Matscheg and Giacomo Spiera. Further proof of this is provided by an incident that took place in 1815, on the occasion of a visit by Emperor Franz I of Austria, which actually led to the removal of the floor in the Scuola della Misericordia to the Libreria Sansoviniana in Piazza San Marco. This shows that buildings were no longer thought of as single, harmonious units in which every detail had its precise semantic value. It will therefore come as no surprise to learn that in 1896 Baron Giorgio Franchetti personally constructed a superb floor at Ca' d'Oro that re-interpreted the ones in St Mark's and San Donato, after he had obtained ancient materials from wherever he could find them.

As we come nearer to our own era, the gap between past and present widens. Nevertheless, there are still outstanding artists who are capable of laying to one side the language of the past and creating a new idiom with traditional materials. The greatest of these is Carlo Scarpa, as is evident from the floor of the former Olivetti shop in Piazza San Marco and that in the Fondazione Scientifica Querini Stampalia.

And so we come to the end of this brief survey. Our aim, apart from providing an introduction to this volume, has been to show how the history of Venetian art and architecture can be read from its floors and pavings. What follows is a closer examination of these near-forgotten jewels.

The floor of St Mark's Basilica may be considered emblematic of the entire city. The alterations it has undergone since 1071, the year cited by Francesco Sansovino as that in which the present building was erected, reflect those that have taken place in the fabric of Venice itself. It has always been a source of inspiration for the designs used in other floors.

Porta di San Pietro
The perfect geometrical figure of the starred dodecahedron, attributed by Michelangelo Muraro to Paolo Uccello and executed between 1425 and 1430, denotes the entrance to the sacred edifice and alludes to the other dodecahedron at the beginning of the presbytery. The motif is framed by concentric circles and diamonds in *opus sectile* decorated with abstract patterns in *opus tessellatum*.

South Transept
The large lapis lazuli stone in the middle of the circle is surrounded by a series of concentric bands delimiting *opus sectile* triangles that generate three-dimensional patterns and perspective effects. The circle is framed by a band of hexagonal polyhedrons and inserted into an *opus tessellatum* square decorated with stylized floral motifs.

North Aisle
The small, flat-surfaced triangles that decorate the floor symmetrically are modern replacements for the ancient, convex tesserae that can still be found in the great octagons of the right-hand aisle. Between one octagon and the other, two pairs of peacocks, the symbol of immortality, turn to the vase in the centre holding the Tree of Life.

North Aisle
The red-and-white plant motif on a black background in *opus tessellatum* and the three heraldic eagles were relaid in 1522 when Jacopo Sansovino reinforced the pillars supporting the domes. The original iconography was scrupulously maintained, but sixteenth-century mosaic techniques were used. Fragments of the original eagles are conserved in the epigraphic museum of Sant'Apollonia.

29

North Transept
The panel showing the burial of a fox was relaid in 1623 by Alberto Parise. At the end of the sixteenth century, Francesco Sansovino offered a historical interpretation of such panels: "most of these represent future events, precepts or admonitions." The two cockerels bearing a fox on their shoulders are thought to symbolize two kings of France, Charles VIII and Louis XII, carrying Ludovico Sforza, nicknamed 'the Fox' because of his cunning, away from the state of Milan. The floor in front of the Mascoli Chapel was renovated more recently. The flower that may be seen today was the original motif, as is clear from drawings by Visentini dated 1761 and Moretti dated 1881. The rhinoceros replaced an earlier sunburst design. In his guide, Antoine Pasini wrote that traces of this motif survived in the legs of the rhinoceros and the trunk of the tree.

Chapel of the Madonna Nicopeia
The panels, which certainly predate 1500, comprise a series of rectangles inlaid with porphyry, lapis lazuli, malachite and chalcedony. In 1502 they were described by Marc'Antonio Sabellico in his *Del sito di Venezia città*: "The floor is covered partly in stones and partly in slabs of marble and other materials of no little price, and even (though this is scarcely credible) stones of chalcedony half a foot long can be noted."

North Transept
In the middle of the huge inlaid floor is a shield of red, green and blue triangles converging on a centre made up of four modern porphyry rosettes. The originals are in the epigraphic museum of Sant'Apollonia.

Presbytery
At the top of the steps in the presbytery, a slab of red Cattaro marble encloses three geometrically defined circles.

Presbytery
A lapis lazuli stone
surrounded by alternating
bands of Parian marble and
opus sectile defines the
lateral figures on the floor
panel. A three-dimensional
dodecahedron emerges
from the central element, its
privileged position
underlining the 'divine'
nature of mathematics.

Presbytery
To the left of the high altar,
a heart-shaped panel in
Verona marble bears a ducal
hat and a hedgehog, to
indicate the spot where the
heart of Francesco Erizzo,
doge from 1633 to 1644, is
buried in a porcelain urn.
The urn was found intact
during restoration work in
1964.

Presbytery

Behind the ciborium and under the Pala d'Oro, an *opus sectile* cushion made up of small 'pelta' shields in precious marble represents the waves of the sea. It is a rare example of a recurrent motif, also featured as early as AD 579 in the church of Sant'Eufemia at Grado, although there it is executed in *opus tessellatum*.

South Transept
Despite modern restoration, this section of flooring is seriously damaged because it was relaid in soft marble that has poor resistance to wear and tear. In contrast, the parts that are still in the original materials are not only more durable but also more attractive. In the second intercolumnar space, the *opus tessellatum* panel is a symmetrical, abstract, floral composition in red and black. Four birds are perched on the branches, two of them contrasting with the golden yellow background almost as if they were about to fly off.

previous pages
South Transept
During restoration work by
Ferdinando Forlati in the
1960s, it was discovered
that the sunburst floral
motif was the cover of
a well dating from the
Romanesque period. The
120-cm-diameter aperture
was probably located
on the site of an earlier,
smaller well.

Baptistery
The diamond-, square-
and triangle-based pattern
in semi-precious marble,
alluding to the motifs in
the chapel of the Madonna
Nicopeia, enhances the
perspectives of the
hexagonal, chequered
design around the base of
the baptismal font. The
floor was laid in 1545,
when Jacopo Sansovino
was *proto*, or supervisor,
of St Mark's Basilica.

following pages
North Transept
The rosette in concentric
porphyry and serpentine
motifs in the right-hand
intercolumnar space of the
north transept is a perfect
example of recent
restoration.

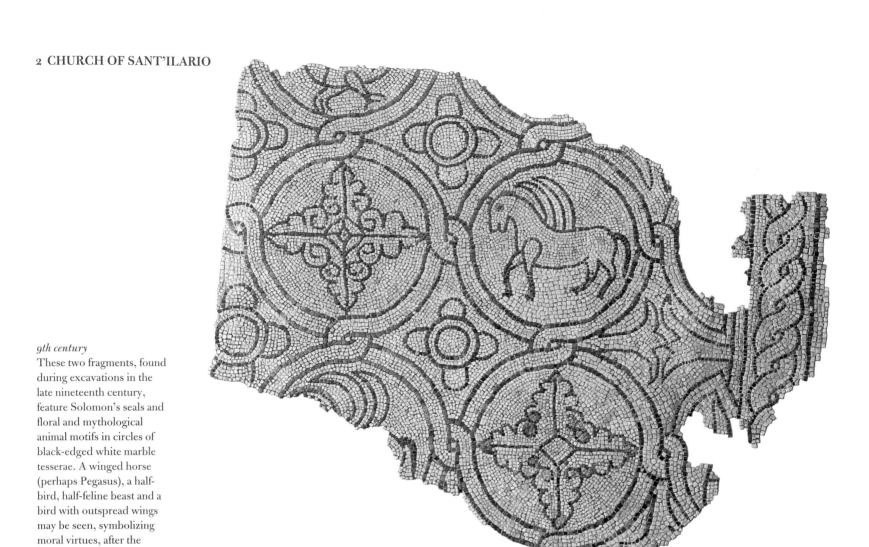

9th century
These two fragments, found during excavations in the late nineteenth century, feature Solomon's seals and floral and mythological animal motifs in circles of black-edged white marble tesserae. A winged horse (perhaps Pegasus), a half-bird, half-feline beast and a bird with outspread wings may be seen, symbolizing moral virtues, after the manner of the medieval bestiaries.

Late 12th century
Discovered at a depth of
175 cm during recent
structural consolidation,
these fragments of *opus
tessellatum*, especially the
inscription between the two
series of arches, bear witness
to the fact that the original
floor was relaid.

1141
The date on which the floor was laid is indicated in the inscription *in nomine domini nostri jesu christi anno domini mcxli mense septembri indictione v* (In the name of our Lord, Jesus Christ, in the month of September in the year 1141) in large black letters on a white band of *opus tessellatum* around an *opus sectile* core set in the very centre of the nave. Half-hidden in the north aisle is a small mosaic Star of David, symbolizing the continuity between the Old Testament and the New. Diamonds of grey porphyry, alternating with identical figures and small black and white squares in the same material, form the basic pattern of the bands framing the large white slabs of the nave flooring.

Sixty-four squares of black and white mosaic form a chessboard in the fourth intercolumnar space of the south aisle. The same motif may be seen in the cathedral at Otranto as well as in the lower cathedral of Pesaro. Chess, which became popular in the West only in the eleventh and twelfth centuries, was symbolic of wisdom in the Arab world. At the entrance to the south apse, the clean red and black lines of a Solomon's seal stand out against a white background.

It is only in the church of Santi Maria e Donato that we find a pair of basilisks, half-cockerel and half-lizard, in a heraldic position in front of the Tree of Life, as in typical pagan iconography.

As in St Mark's Basilica and the church of San Lorenzo, the panel with twin mirror-image arcades separated by a series of small squares and diamonds forms a sort of artist's signature, marking completion of the floor.

The abstract figures that came to light in the north arm of the transept may represent mating ants – probably symbolizing the birth of religion and the growth of the Church – or, as Marilyn Perry has suggested, two gigantic crickets smelling a flower.

The eagle, queen of the skies, composed in precious tesserae of *opus vermiculatum*, is portrayed clutching its prey in its claws. The breast feathers are drawn so as to resemble a coat of armour.

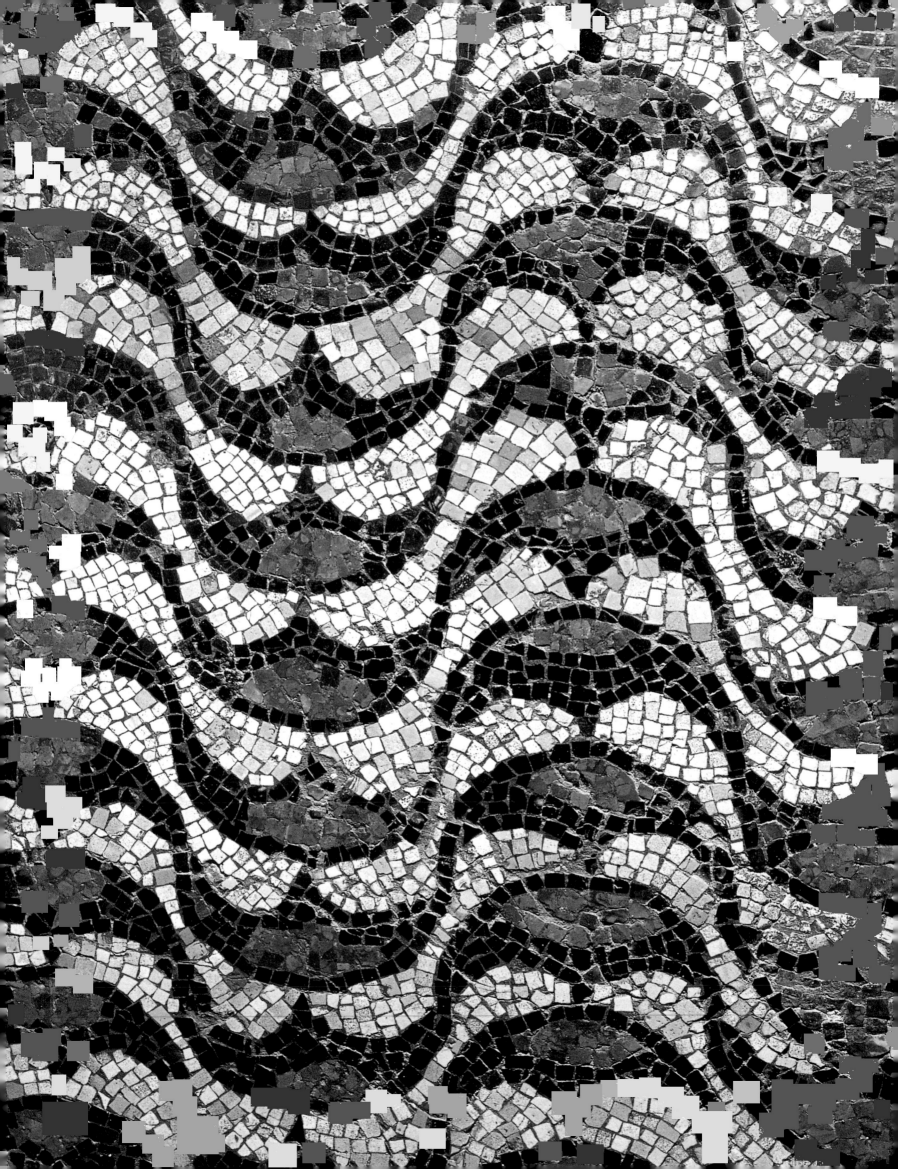

The classic wave motif, taken from late classical mosaics, can also be found at Murano as *opus tessellatum*. The small, roughly drawn maze in recycled stone and rubble situated in the north arm of the transept is reminiscent of five similar contemporary designs on the floor of the church at Der Sharqi in Syria.

1176
The floor of what is today the chapel of San Tarasio features a sunburst motif made up of triangular elements spreading out from a central point on the chord of the apse. The various birds on the white background include a reddish mallard, picked out by an outline of black tesserae, which is taking to the air. On each side of the altar are the surviving fragments of an eagle and two fawns, representing the immortality of the soul and faith in God.

6 BASILICA OF SANTA MARIA ASSUNTA AT TORCELLO

Second half of 12th century
The floor, comparable to those in St Mark's and San Donato, is the only one with no figurative elements. It was probably the result of a design that was carefully drawn and then rapidly executed. Like a jewel set in a ring, the composite Eastern marble cushion lies in a lace-like black-and-white pattern, held in place on the green porphyry by four triangular 'clips'.

following pages
The floor of the choir picks up the *opus sectile* motif of a circle set in a square from St Mark's and San Donato, where the blacks, reds, yellows, whites and light greys of Eastern marble, especially porphyry and serpentine, dominate the tesserae of the panels. In the interstices, small triangles, squares, diamonds and abstract flowers in *opus sectile* with occasional mosaic inserts, some in gilt glass, form an endlessly repeated pattern.

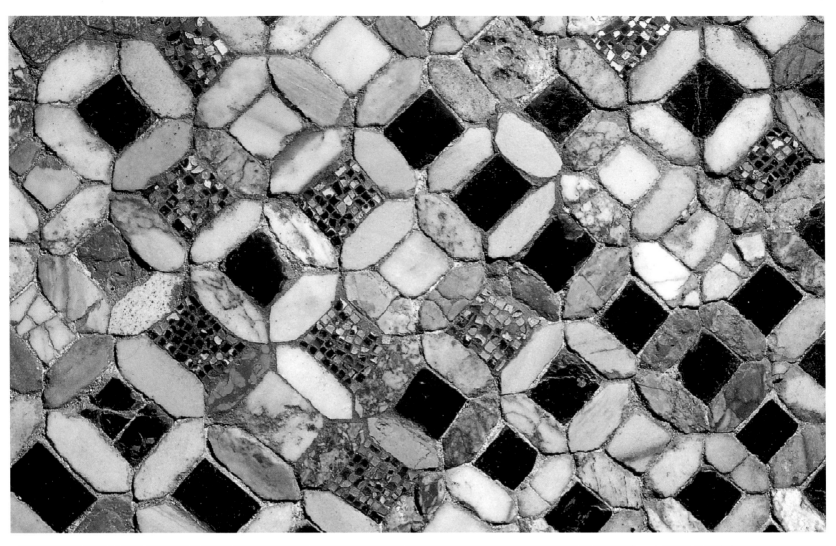

6 BASILICA OF SANTA MARIA ASSUNTA AT TORCELLO

In the middle of the nave, an elaborate floral motif set in concentric circles may well indicate, as in St Mark's, the site of the ancient well.

In the nave, at the foot of the choir, a pattern of diagonal lines in *opus sectile* creates elaborate geometrical figures inspired by Arab and Sicilian floors from the Romanesque period.

7 CAMPO DELLA MADONNA DELL'ORTO

Second half of 14th century
The herring-bone pattern of bricks set in large squares delineated by strips of white Istrian stone is one of the most ancient kinds of Venetian external paving. Piazza San Marco was also paved like this from 1264 to 1723, as can be seen in the 1496 *telero* by Gentile Bellini, the *Procession of the Cross in the Piazza San Marco*.

Mid-15th century

Until 1885, Venice's water supply relied mainly on wells. It was therefore crucial for every palazzo to have one, which was usually located in the middle of the courtyard. The paving had a dual purpose, both functional and decorative. The white inserts in Istrian stone against the background of herring-bone brick highlight the perimeter of the cistern and the rainwater conduits.

1489
A long aisle of precious
marble, into which
tombstones have
subsequently been inserted,
links the main entrance to
the steps leading up to the
presbytery. The design is a
grid pattern of Greek
cipollino, Carrara, pink
Verona and black Isea
marble.

In the centre of the presbytery, roundels of serpentine and porphyry, set in a surface of grey paonazzetto marble and surrounded by elements in alternating colours, form a Venetian example of Cosmati work. Set to the sides in precise symmetry are *trompe l'œil* designs in Torri and Mori yellow, Belgian black and various kinds of Verona marble. Restoration work carried out in 1887 and 1970 has in places substituted the black marble with slabs of slate.

Despite the extensive restoration and restructuring of the Scuola Tedesca, the original sixteenth-century floor has survived and performs a vitally important architectural function. The two rosettes set in the foci of the ellipse, a projection of the women's gallery overhead, frame the *tevà*, which today stands against the wall opposite the *aròn*. Originally it was located in the middle of the hall under the lantern. The half-rosettes on the two longitudinal walls mark off the space set aside for prayer benches. The shape of the women's gallery, and the optical illusion created by the light flooding in to be reflected on the pattern on the floor, manage to lend geometrical unity to an unusually configured, trapezoidal room. The rhythmical body movements characteristic of Jewish prayer imbue the rosettes with an elliptical dynamic that spirals towards the centre.

1591–96

In the warm atmosphere of the interior, dominated by white plaster, the floor provides the only note of colour in a design scheme that varies depending on the function of the space delimited. In the presbytery area, the perspective effect of white, grey and black diamonds of marble creates the illusion of a relief surface, as if underlining the fact that the presbytery stands three steps above the level of the church. In the choir, which was reserved for the monks, the inlaid floor presents star patterns in red, black and grey marble on a white background, similar to the floor painted by Jacopo Tintoretto in the *Last Supper* hanging in the presbytery.

previous pages
1676–83
In *L'isola e il cenobio di San Giorgio Maggiore*, Gino Damerini notes that, between 1676 and 1683, when Pietro Sagredo was abbot of the Benedictine monastery, "the piazza in front of the façade was paved in Monselice stone (trachyte)". Visually, the pattern in Istrian stone is stunningly effective with its succession of interweaving octagons.

1644

The sumptuous, monumental, double staircase is the most theatrical creation of Baldassare Longhena, the architect who inspired the high period of Venetian Baroque. The scenic impact and perspective effects generated by this imposing structure are enhanced by the designs of the floor and landings, which are also probably by Longhena. At the foot of the central flight, the floor has alternate octagons of Istrian stone and pink Verona marble. The square-shaped interstices are in black African marble. In contrast, the landings give ample space to abstract patterns. The central landing features an eight-pointed geometrical flower, while the two lateral flights have identical, more traditional motifs: a double black-and-white marble star in a white square edged with red Verona marble.

IOSEPHI · I
INTER · SPLENDIDA · UR
D · GEORGII · CO
UNA · CUM · FRATRIB
INVISENT
ANNO · MDCCLXXV
MONUMENT

13 CHURCH OF THE REDENTORE

In a sort of reflection of the lines of the façade on the grey *masegno* paving, the white lines of Istrian stone delimit the area belonging to the church, highlighting its sacred nature. The design, too, is carefully calculated, each of the geometrical figures representing one of the areas of the interior. The large central diamond bordered by four triangles symbolizes the nave while the two lateral rectangles represent the side chapels.

1616

The simplicity of the red-and-white diamond floor in the nave contrasts with the richly decorated flooring in the area of the presbytery, which on feast days was set aside for political and ecclesiastical dignitaries. The presbytery floor, illuminated by light coming from the lantern and the sides, is a projection of the structure overhead. The circular shape, set in a square, is a kaleidoscope of colours, the grey African, white Carrara and red Cattaro marble contrasting with the black Belgian marble background to create a relief effect. A meander, again in Carrara and pink Verona marble, links the lateral semicircles.

The external paving in straight rows of *masegno* trachyte and Istrian stone features a circle-and-rectangle-based geometrical pattern that corresponds to the walls of the chapels inside the church and to the volumes of the buttresses. The *masegno* blocks, which are laid edge to edge, are trimmed to fit the decorative motif they were intended to fill.

The entire church resembles a vast crown, the shape that Baldassare Longhena held to be suitable for a building dedicated to the Virgin Mary. The floor is a projection of the structure and spreads out in concentric circles from the inscription in the central rosette – *unde origo, inde salus mdcxxxi* – in commemoration of the legendary date of the city's foundation on 25 March 421, the feast of the Annunciation. A broad decorative strip creates a perspective effect of diamonds, triangles, circles and squares in various kinds of marble, from red Verona and yellow Torri to black Iseo and white Carrara.

The inlaid-marble central tondo is surrounded by five roses, the symbol par excellence of the Virgin, and by five buds in broccatello marble, Verona flame yellow and green Alpine marble stalks inlaid on a background of white Carrara. The floral motif recurs in the thirty-three roses – the same number as the years of Christ's life – in the outside circular segments, which are filled with diamond shapes in shades of white, yellow, red and black. In contrast, the presbytery is decorated with a diamond-based perspective effect in black, red and white marble. The original sketches for both designs, attributed to Baldassare Longhena, are extant.

19 CHURCH OF SAN NICOLÒ DA TOLENTINO

The external paving was executed by Andrea Tirali in 1706–14. It features composite geometrical figures in Istrian stone on a background of Euganean trachyte *masegno* laid edge to edge, which enhances and adds perspective to the long, narrow portico running from the colonnade to the façade. The abundant curving white lines soften the rigour of the Neo-classical façade. In the chapel of the Pisani family and the chapel of the Corner family, two of the many chapels inside the church, the clearly Palladian-inspired floors feature a late sixteenth-century central star design set in a large frame with mirror-image geometrical motifs on each of the four sides. The colours are achieved through the use of precious marble, such as white Carrara, green serpentine, black Iseo, red Verona and yellow Torri.

1710

Although the original designs of the floor have been lost, the solutions adopted enable it to be attributed to Antonio Gaspari. It was Gaspari who finished work on the palazzo after the death of Baldassare Longhena, the original architect, who did not live to see his project completed. The ground-floor entrance hall is characterized by a pink floor in Verona stone on which is traced a white marble maze, an unusual motif in Venice. Light reflected from the Grand Canal lends movement to the design, illuminating the space, which is extended on to the landing through the use of the same colour scheme. The floors of the upper landings are decorated in pink on a multicoloured background, which softens into delicate floral motifs near the windows.

21 PALAZZO TREVISAN MORO

Early 18th century
The library of Palazzo Trevisan Moro has the only floor in Venice with an Eastern theme. The *chinoiserie* motifs, which were extremely popular in Venice during the eighteenth century, are set on a bed of ochre-coloured terracotta scattered with white chippings. The lily-like decorative groups feature palm trees, pagodas, birds and tropical vegetation in various kinds of marble, including black Iseo and yellow Torri, as well as grey and red Verona. Dragonflies, butterflies and salamanders provide linking elements between one decorative motif and the next, and the delicacy of their execution enriches and enhances this highly original floor.

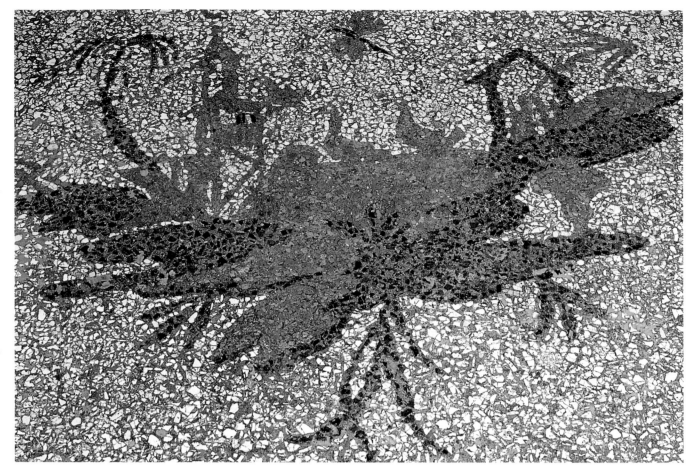

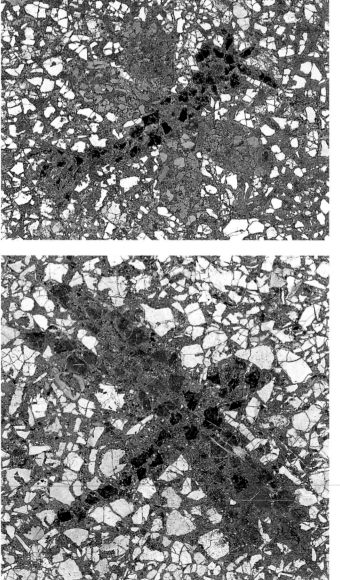

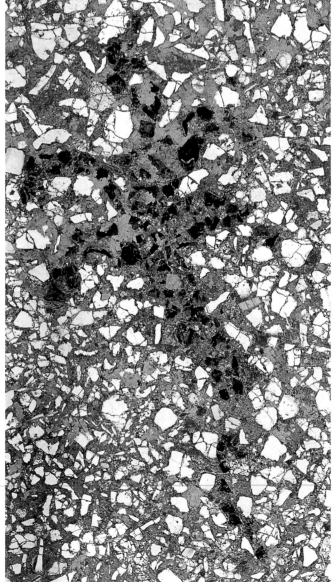

On the ground floor, against a background of lime and terracotta, a meander interspersed with floral motifs frames abstract shoots in green Alpine marble bearing fruit in yellow Siena. Tulips in various shades of red Verona and yellow Torri marble are scattered over a field in white chippings.

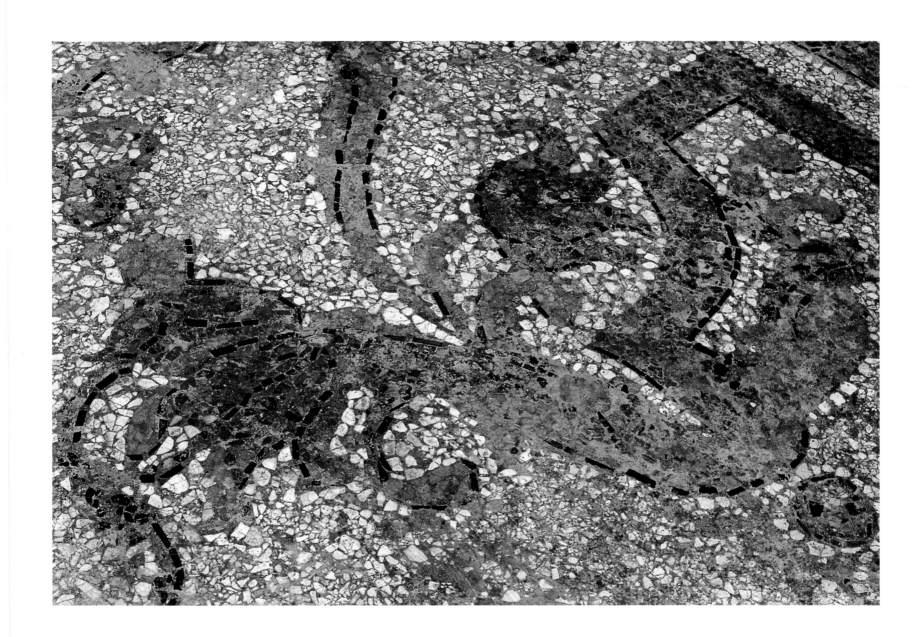

A finely detailed embroidery in bardiglio on white marble provides a sophisticated and original contrast.

About 1738
The success of Domenico Rossi's floor in the church of the Gesuiti induced Giorgio Massari to opt for a geometric floor design in Istrian stone and grey-blue bardiglio marble for this unlucky and still-incomplete church. The architect, who took great care over the details and finish, laid down a pattern of diamonds and composite figures, the optical effect of which corrects the misalignment of the two entrances to the church with respect to the high altar.

D · O · M ·
NICOLAO BALBI
THOMÆ FILIO
SENATORI AMPLISSIMO
HUJUS ECCLESIÆ PROCUR. OPTIME MERITO
RELIGIONI, PATRIÆ, LITTERIS
APPRIME CHARO
FATO FUNCTO XIV. KAL. FEBR.
ÆTATIS SUÆ ANNO LXXXI
MŒRENTES FILII
SIBI ET POSTERIS.
ANNO A.N.D.
MDCCXCI

25 CASIN DETTO DEL BAFFO

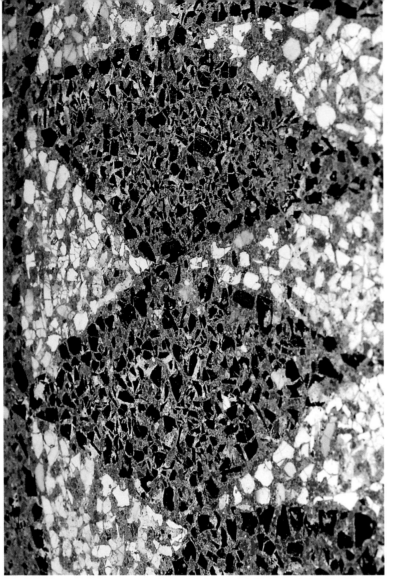

1730
The floor decoration of the two side rooms is characterized by circular figures set off-centre towards the windows. One of these circles is formed by twenty-two black diamond-shaped spatulas, each joined to the centre by a line, on a background of white chippings. In the middle of the floor in the main room on the second floor, under a harlequin pattern of scattered chippings, is a large peony bearing the date when the floor was laid. Its petals are picked out in black Iseo marble. Again the background is in white chippings.

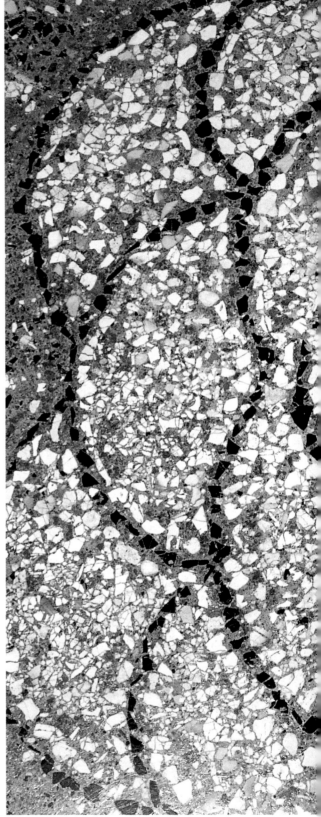

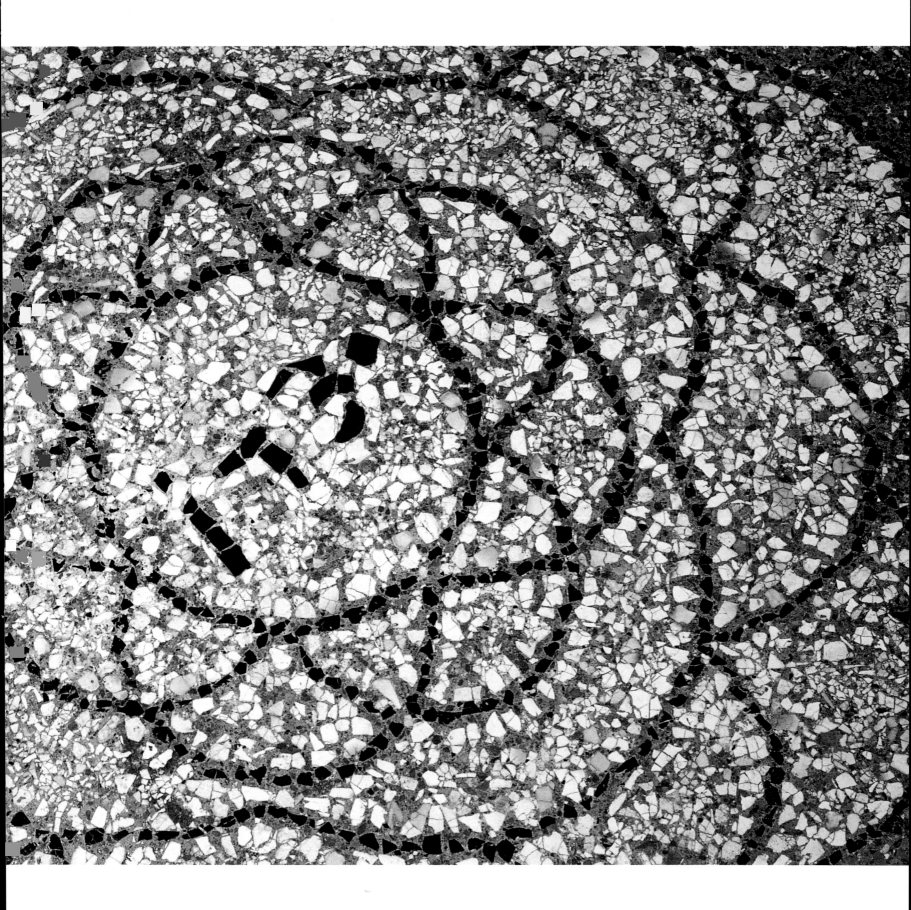

1740

In the hall of the hostel, the double compass in white Carrara and red Verona marble is enclosed by an ellipse in black Belgian marble and edged by bands and squares in composite Eastern marble. Around it, other geometrical figures create perspective effects in classic Venetian colours: red Verona, white Trani and grey bardiglio marble, which are also the colours in the diamonds in the corridor. The floors on the landings of the elegant staircase, probably built to a design by Antonio Gaspari, feature a motif drawn from the endless examples to be found in the floors of St Mark's.

1742

The floors of the mezzanine were executed by the *terrazer* Bortolo Cecchin, to a design by Gerolamo Mengozzi, called Il Colonna. An oval flower with yellow Torri marble petals in a sinuously curved pink Verona marble medallion stands out impressively against the sparsely scattered white-chipping background in the reception room of Caterina Sagredo Barbarigo's apartment. In 1766 Caterina installed herself in the suite after the death of her husband. As a visible expression of her grief, she had a pierced heart added to the design. To the sides of the central rosette in the living-room are the crests of the Sagredo and Barbarigo families, set in a double cartouche in black and various shades of Verona marble.

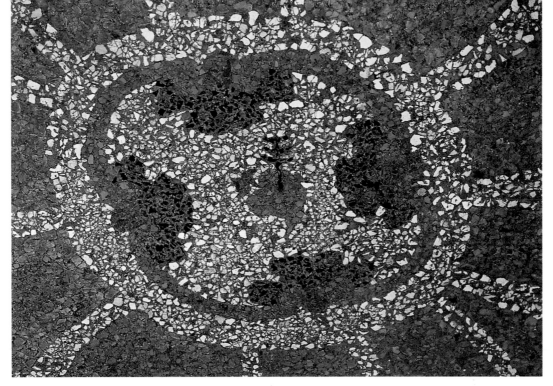

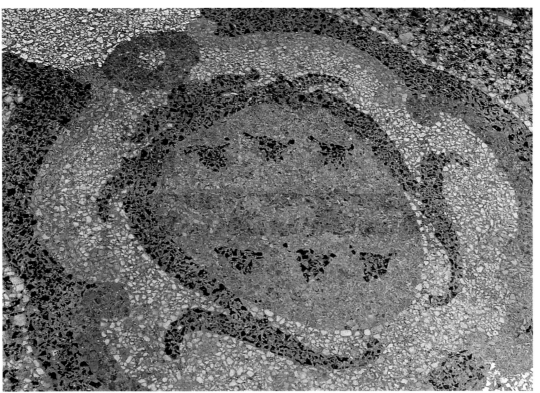

The terrazzo floor in the corner room, marked off by a broad diamond-motif cushion, is surrounded by elaborate wreaths.

28 PALAZZO PISANI MORETTA

1742–45

The present floors were designed by Francesco Zanchi, the *proto* who was entrusted with the restoration work commissioned by Chiara Pisani, and laid by the *terrazeri* Domenico and Giacomo Crovato. The marble-inlay landings feature a number of ornamental motifs. On the first landing, a background of Greek Parian marble bears an abstract daisy in yellow Mori, black Iseo and red Cattaro marble. The second landing has an elaborate, perspective-enhancing design in which a ribbon of lapis lazuli-adorned red French marble encloses a tiny sun at the centre of an ellipse. Its sinuous, black-edged outer strips in bardiglio stone enclose irregular shapes with yellow Siena floral details. The edges of the slabs that form the background reveal that they were recovered from ancient columns. The third landing floor is made up of vividly coloured, strongly contrasting diamonds and tetrahedrons in an elegant pink background that resembles a gold-embroidered silk cape.

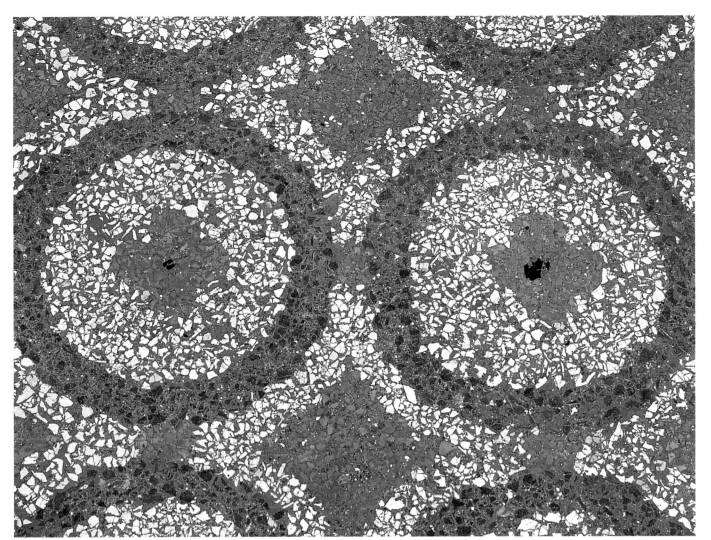

The floor in the Apollo room has a tightly packed design of bardiglio circles, and flowers and diamonds in yellow Mori marble on a background of white chippings. It is decorated in the corners and on the centre line with floral motifs in the same materials.

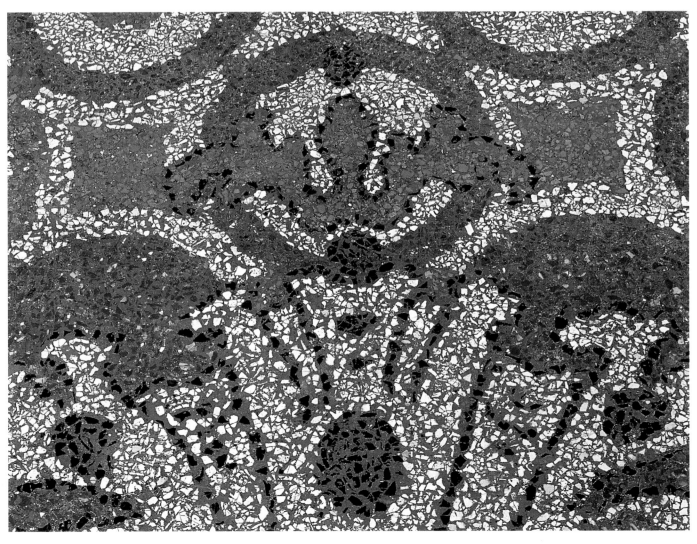

Early 16th century

The courtyard was probably laid to a design by Sante Lombardo. It is paved in characteristic slabs of Euganean trachyte *masegno* and features a well set in an octagon of Istrian stone. Radii join the centre of the octagon to the eight corners, marking off the well area. Rainwater was collected in the four circular drainage conduits, also in Istrian stone.

Even though the palazzo dates from the Renaissance, the floor decorations, in terrazzo on a lime bed, were executed during the radical restructuring work carried out in the mid-eighteenth century. One of the most striking subjects is the Piovene family crest in the Sala delle Allegorie, featuring a red French marble lion rampant with a yellow Torri crown on a background of white chippings. The floor of the corner room overlooking the Grand Canal boasts a beautifully executed copy of a late classical mosaic. Neptune, brandishing a trident, is galloping on a grey charger with large fins instead of front hoofs. Before him, a Triton is sounding a conch, while a bag, perhaps the one containing favourable winds, can be seen half-hidden by the horse's tail fins. The scene probably celebrates the exploits of the Piovene family, one of whose ancestors, Guido, was a lieutenant-general of cavalry who died heroically during the siege of Nicosia in 1570.

About 1772
The bands of Istrian stone in the courtyard highlight the drainage conduits and mark off the well. Diamond-shaped figures embellish the surface and decorate the courtyard as if it were a room with leaf-clad walls. Inside, the sumptuous floor of the corner room, which extends over 88 square metres, is framed by a double band of diamonds and lozenges in black Iseo and green Alpine marble, intertwined with floral patterns in granulated yellow Torri and red Cattaro marble in the French idiom. The background of granulated white *ciottolo* chippings bears the outline of four geometrical figures decorated with red Cattaro plumes on a background of lapis lazuli-studded bardiglio. A white line enhances the golden yellow edge decorated with a sunburst pattern of green foliage.

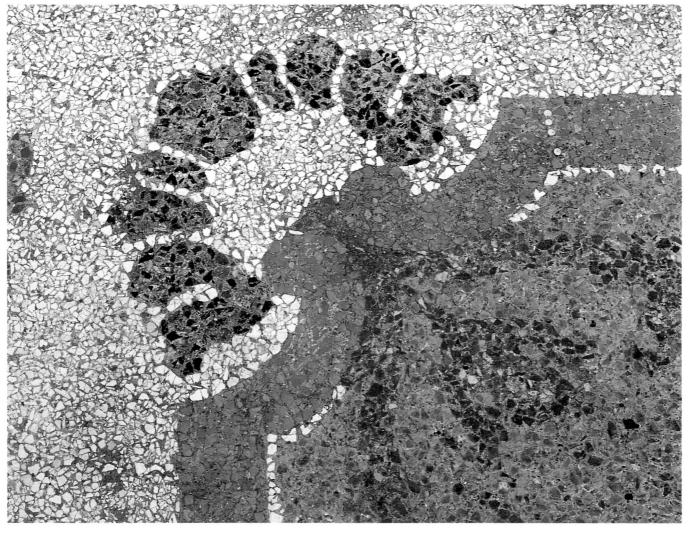

1755–66
The floors in the Sala del Capitolo and on the landings may be attributed to Bernardino Maccaruzzi, and were completed during the extensive restructuring carried out in the mid-eighteenth century. The vast hall, inspired by St Mark's, has a background of grey, black and white, over which predominates a network of criss-crossing broken lines generating various geometrical figures. One of these is the unusual motif of superimposed flowers, created either by using several different kinds of brightly coloured marble or by juxtaposing white Trani marble with broccato from Verona. The perfectly symmetrical landing, with its twelve-pointed star-shaped flower motif, is more traditional in conception.

The remainder of the flooring from the Great Hall of the Scuola della Misericordia was used for the Sala Dorata. A sequence of Carrara marble squares was laid diagonally in a grid of green Calabrian marble and parangon from Gorizia. On this stand the display cabinets containing the institution's rarest books and manuscripts, including the renowned Grimani Breviary.

The interior of Palazzo Loredan has undergone a number of restructuring interventions, the first of which, commissioned by Doge Francesco Loredan, took place in 1760, the year when the floor in the dressing-room was laid. The room's stuccoed walls are continued in the edges of the floor, and the delicate perimeter decoration echoes the cornice of the ceiling. The golden yellow surface in the centre completes the mirror effect by alluding to the fresco overhead.

In 1807, when the palazzo was the residence of the first
French governor of Venice, General Baraguay d'Hilliers,
the room that is now the library was transformed. The
floor became one great expanse of golden yellow, into
which was set a single cornice decorated with large, white,
grey-edged petals, in the style of the time.

1770–75

The terrazzo floor of the main reception room alludes to the stuccoes that surround the central fresco on the ceiling. Four curlicued concentric fascias, in alternating yellow Torri and red Verona marble, enclose the white-dotted rosette with interwoven flowers in bardiglio, yellow Torri, green Alpine and red Cattaro marble. Volutes embellish the space between the fascias. The mirror dressing-room floor, in contrast, has a geometrical motif designed to deceive the eye. Interwoven garlands in yellow Torri marble enclose a daisy, marking off an elaborate, diamond-themed composition in white chippings, grey Karst and red Verona. The living-room floor has a harlequin pattern made from pieces of marble cut by hand using a technique that was unique to Venice and employed only in special circumstances because of its high cost. Mother-of-pearl inserts further enhance the impact.

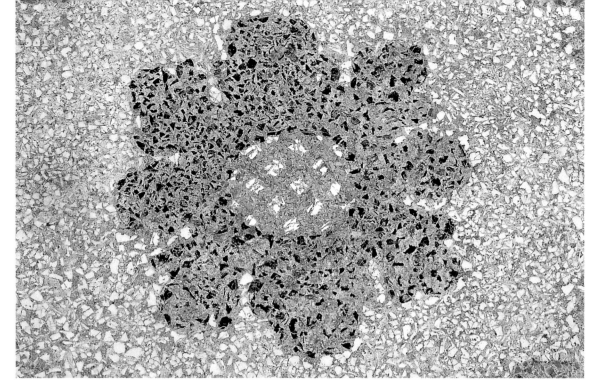

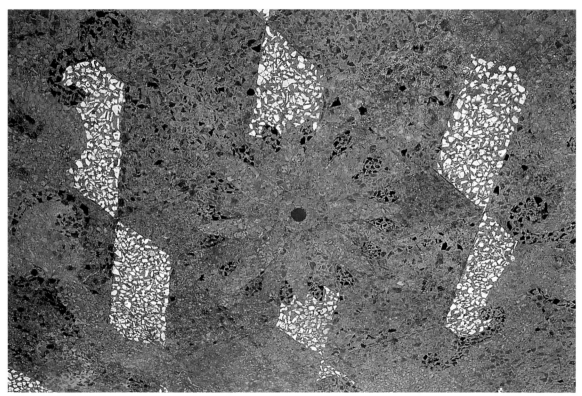

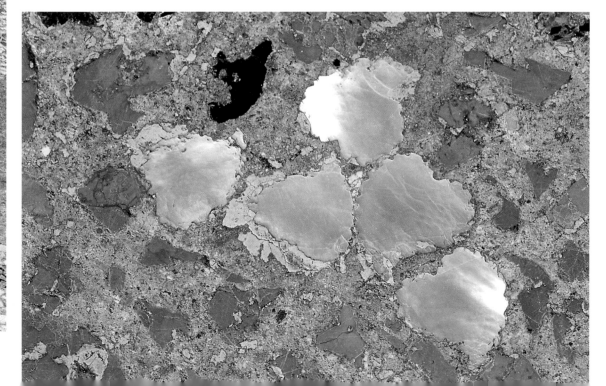

1776

The room overlooking the canal has a terrazzo floor on a background of white chippings and a profiled ribbon in red Verona marble with black edging. In the middle is a parrot, the symbol of wisdom. Its body is in black Iseo marble, the feathers are lapis lazuli blue and the eye is mother-of-pearl, and the bird is perched on a branch bearing exotic fruit in pink Verona marble. The motifs testify to the Oriental tastes that were the fashion of the day.

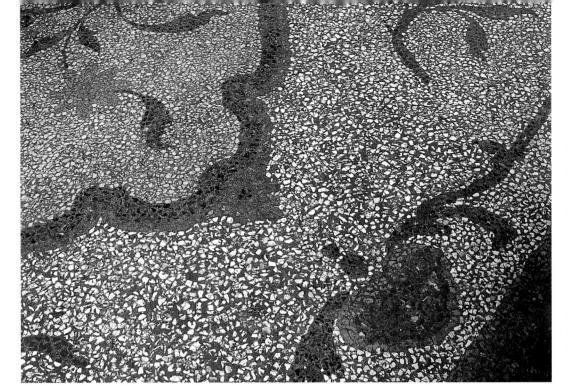

Second half of 18th century
The piano nobile of this sixteenth-century building was restructured in the late eighteenth century. The stuccoed rooms feature terrazzo floors that allude to the decorations on the walls and ceilings. The earliest of the floors, in the part of the entrance corridor that looks on to the courtyard, has a light-coloured background with a central motif of arabesques forming a delicate tracery. In the corner room, the floor of which was laid some years later, the central motif is a small, asymmetrical garden of rocks and flowers. There is a frog, the symbol of fertility, and a gnarled tree laden with red berries in the foreground. A pelican, the symbol of abundance, soars aloft.

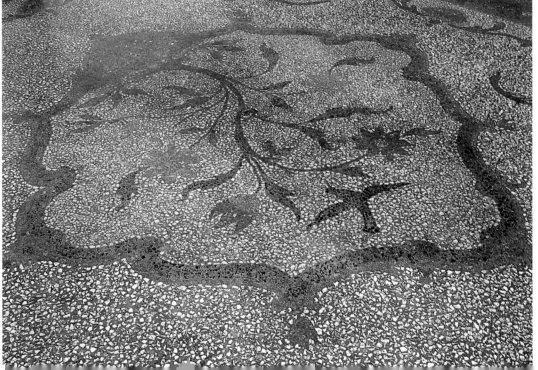

1788

The largest – 6 square metres – and most richly ornate family crest in Venice is to be found in the palazzo where Lord Byron stayed. Framed in a ribbon of granulated black Iseo marble and lapis lazuli, and fronds of pink Verona and red Prugna marble, the design features lapis lazuli inserts and gold mosaic tesserae in the crown. The main background is picked out in two shades of chippings, white and grey, on which are two roses, the symbol of the Mocenigo family.

42 PALAZZO MOCENIGO AT SAN STAE

1787
A typical eighteenth-century noble residence, Palazzo Mocenigo at San Stae has preserved its furnishings intact, including two exquisitely decorated floors. In the green room, a white background bears the family crest, depicted in a mixture of various kinds of marble, including red Cattaro, black Belgian and green Alpine. The design is brightened by attractive inserts in mother-of-pearl, lapis lazuli and gold mosaic tesserae. The floor in the red room is a sumptuous design on a bed of lime and crushed terracotta, with elegant floral motifs in white chippings, green Alpine and coral red Verona marble, set in frames of grey African marble.

43 HOUSE AT SANTO STEFANO

About 1830
Confirmation that this building used to belong to the Cavalli family comes from the stunning crest on the ground floor. Complete with plumes, halberds, flags and two horses, the coat of arms sits resplendent in red, grey and black marble in the centre of the white-chipping entrance-hall floor.

141

1858
The glass mosaic floor was probably laid to a design by Lodovico Cadorin, who also restructured the premises. It shows, framed in a gold-ribbon surround, an attractive lion of St Mark set between the sea, symbolized by greenish-coloured glass tesserae, and the sky in dark blue tesserae.

45 PALAZZO CAVALLI FRANCHETTI

About 1880
The entrance hall, restructured by Carlo Matscheg, is paved with tapering inlaid marble slabs in dark grey bardiglio, yellow Verona nembro and white secchiaro, the interweaving arrangement of which creates a pattern in an obviously neo-Gothic idiom. The original configuration and the successfully matched colours were deliberately selected to create the illusion of waves, bringing the lapping waters of the Grand Canal right inside the palazzo.

1892
The floor design in the main reception room is marked off by an external fascia in pink Verona marble. Geometrical figures in black-edge grey Karst marble stand out against the white-chipping background. In the centre is a yellow Torri marble cross with four black balls representing the four cardinal points of the compass as well as white petals that echo the colour of the background. The staircase leading up to the second piano nobile is embellished with marble tesserae that indicate the date when the floor was laid.

1890

This palazzo once belonged
to the Cavalli family. It has
undergone restructuring and
conversion, including the
work at the end of the
nineteenth century that gave
the interior its neo-Gothic
flavour. The elegantly
executed flooring in the main
reception room, superbly
restored in 1983, dates from
the same period. It was laid
using the technique of lime-
based terrazzo, with a
sprinkled edging on the
stabilitura, or finishing
layer. The pattern comprises
a vast surface with a
background in very fine
granulated white marble
framed in ribbons of yellow
Torri and edged with a
double row of turquoise
glass mosaic tesserae, the
same material as was used
for the decorative stars.

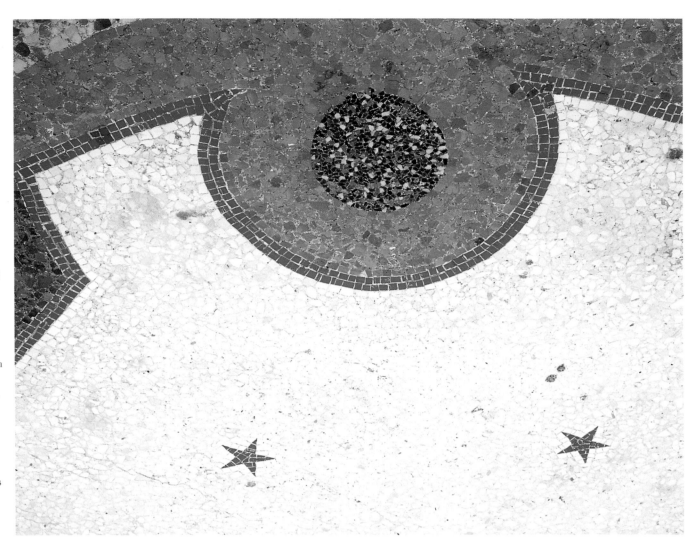

About 1893
The Banca Commerciale
Italiana building is a
characteristic example of
bourgeois Mannerism that
has managed to conserve its
delightful, technically
remarkable floors. The main
reception room on the
second floor has a Neo-
classical design in fine-grain
terrazzo that alludes to the
wooden squares on the
ceiling. The central fascia is
embellished with almonds
in ancient composite
marble, while the
perspective effect inside the
central square, with its star
motif, is obtained by
highlighting in grey the
broken white lines that
generate complex
geometrical figures against
the dark background.

All the floors of the building document for modern observers the formal rationale and superb technique of earlier Venetian marble floors. In the entrance hall, the great central sunburst-pattern star in green Oriental marble echoes the perspective patterns of ancient artisans. The technique of alluding to the mouldings on the ceiling is taken up by the fine-grain terrazzo floor in the central reception room on the upper floor.

Thanks to the use of templates by highly skilled craft workers, the complex execution of the lozenge- and flower-motif design reached a peak of technical and geometrical perfection in the superb 'lace handkerchief', obviously inspired by eighteenth-century models, in the right-hand room. An abstract flower in a lozenge-shaped frame is the hub from which emerge countless spokes of white chippings and an elaborate arabesque.

Acquired in the late nineteenth century by Baron Giorgio
Franchetti, an extraordinary patron of the arts whose ashes
rest under the porphyry memorial stone. Franchetti
purged the building of the heavy neo-Gothic trappings
added by Giambattista Meduna in the mid-eighteenth
century, restoring it to its original nonchalant elegance.
The floors were also completely relaid. Indeed, it seems
that the baron himself, inspired by the mosaics in St
Mark's, personally executed the rich *opus sectile* and *opus
tessellatum* floor on the ground floor.

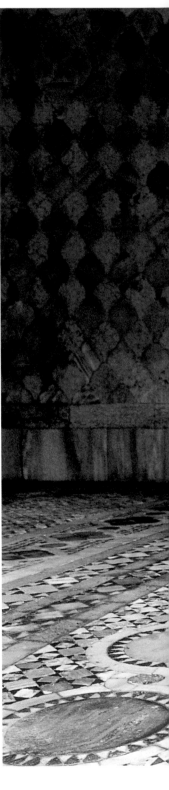

The circle-and-diamond-themed geometrical design with its plate and tondo inserts is a composition of precious marble, mainly from the East, on a mosaic background. Porphyry, serpentine, breccia, fossil-rich lumachella, granite and Parian and Carrara marble were used by the baron as if they were the oils of an artist's palette to 'paint' a coloured pattern of rare beauty. The creation of this masterpiece was observed by, the aesthete and writer Gabriele D'Annunzio, who described it in July 1896 as follows: "I saw, through the shutter on the ground floor, myself bending down with Giorgio Franchetti and Angelo Conti, I saw myself on my knees like a workman inserting porphyry and serpentine in the lime bed to relay the mosaic floor …. We entered …nothing in there had changed. I did not walk on the mosaic, almost as if I were afraid of stepping on my own hands …. The rubble, the boards, the uncut slabs of marble were still there …. We walked in trepidation on the unfinished floor of the Venetian room, restored to its original vastness."

1935
Following an ancient
Venetian tradition, Fabrizio
Clerici, the architect and
designer of the entire edifice,
personally created the
pattern for the flooring, re-
interpreting classic motifs
and incorporating the three
established techniques of
commesso, or marble inlay,
terrazzo and mosaic, linking
them to three separate areas
of the living space. The
terrace features a classic
irregular mosaic floor in
pearl grey stones on a white
background. It reproduces
the sumptuous marble
fronds that decorate the walls
of the church of the Gesuiti.

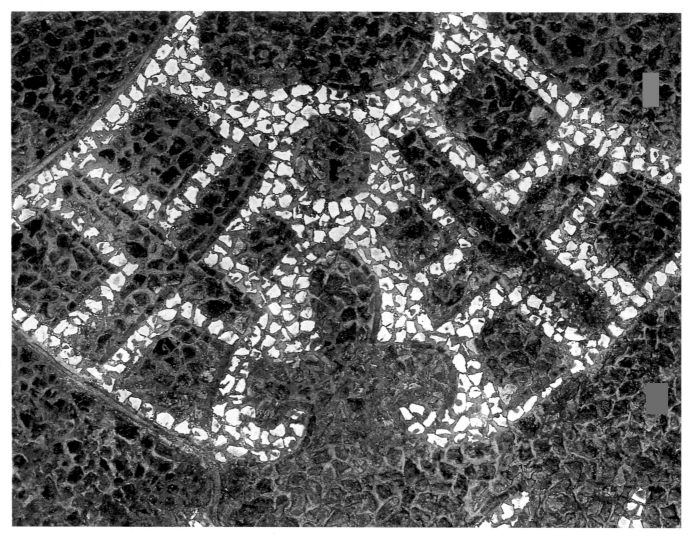

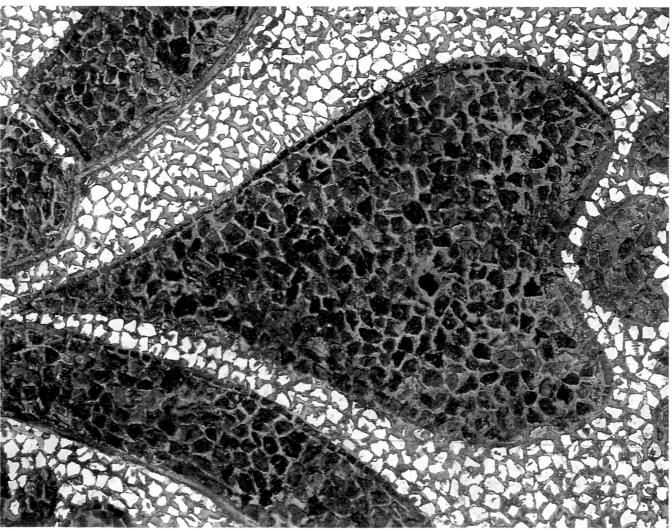

The white-marble-inlay
entrance-hall floor is
embellished with large gilt
floral motifs in an almost
Baroque idiom. The
reception room on the first
floor is in terrazzo. It is
known as the Maggiotto
room, after the allegories of
the twelve months that adorn
its walls. The room also
features a central white
marble star-motif rosette
from which gilt rays emanate,
like the one in the bedroom
apartment at Palazzo Tiepolo
Papadopoli.

The dining-room floor is in terrazzo, the elaborate central star theme being picked up in the decoration of the edging. The gilt inserts and lapis lazuli trim create a delightfully elegant decorative pattern that is repeated on the tabletop. When reflections from the surface of the water filter through the porcelain display cabinets that serve as windows, the marble is illuminated by a continuously changing tracery of light and shade.

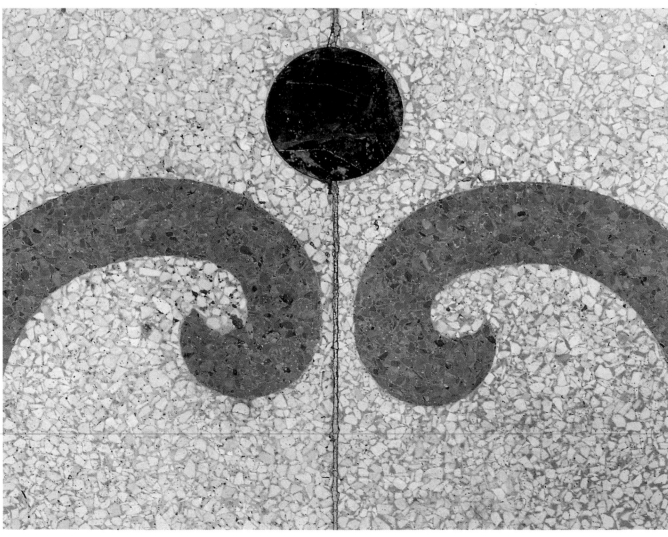

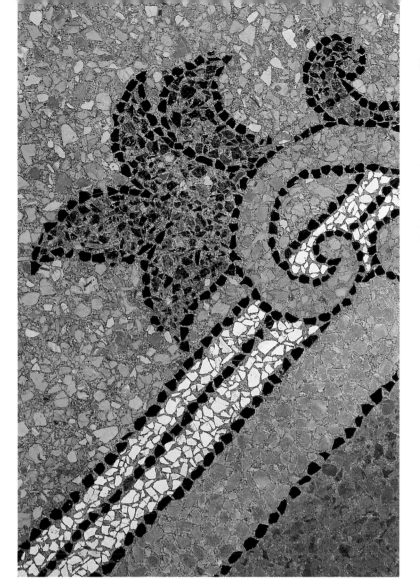

51 HOTEL BAUER GRÜNWALD

1938
In one of the rooms of this modern neo-Gothic building erected by Giovanni Sardi in 1890, we find a sumptuous terrazzo floor in the style of the seventeenth century. It offers a monumental 'tablecloth' that alternates broad swathes of colour with delicate vegetal motifs on a harlequin-pattern background, in red Verona and bardiglio marble.

52 HOTEL CIPRIANI

1956
In one of the hotel suites, there is this plain terrazzo floor with a delicate harlequin pattern in various shades of red Verona marble. Four dolphins winding themselves around tridents, depicted using larger tesserae of Carraro marble, are set in circles to enliven the visual effect.

161

The use of red glass paste tesserae set irregularly in a bed
of light-coloured cement mortar was conjured up by the
superbly skilful Carlo Scarpa to capture and reflect the
light coming in through the extensive shop windows
facing on to Piazza San Marco. When it is covered by
water during the frequent *acqua alta* floods, the floor is
brought to life and is transformed into a gently rippling
mirror reminiscent of certain experimental paintings by
Paul Klee.

1961–63

The age-old quandary faced by Venice is how to protect the city from flooding. Only a Venetian like Carlo Scarpa could have invented a floor that would not merely live but actually merge with the encroaching waters of the lagoon. Scarpa created a highly original configuration of steps and parallel walkways, imitating the ever-shifting nature of the sea in the geometrical floor design that incorporates small squares of different coloured marble, such as pink and plum Verona, white Carrara and green Alpine.

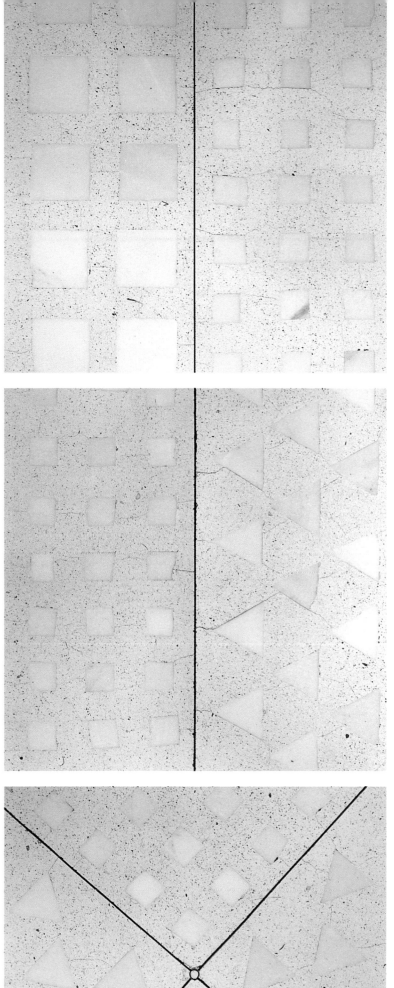

1986
Executed in the ancient terrazzo, or Venetian mosaic, flooring technique, but featuring modern decorative motifs, the floor presents broad bands of triangular and square elements in white Lasa marble, set in a screed of sand-and-cement mortar. The spaces between one decorative figure and the next are in marble chips mixed with cement.

56 PALAZZO ALBRIZZI

1986
The former attic, with its panoramic view over the city, is today the home and retreat of a musician. The floor presents a labyrinthine pattern in soft Vicenza sandstone almost as if it reflects the maze of narrow *calli* below. The smooth, slightly convex meanderings of the design, created by Antonio Foscari and Ferruccio Franzoia, fade away or stand out strongly against the hand-laid *buccellato* background in the shifting light of the sun and rain.

1990

Characteristically Venetian materials such as glass, wood, brick and trachyte set the tone in this meeting point of interior and exterior space. The polished thrust in the entrance of longitudinal lines of trachyte, traditionally used only out of doors, are carried over into the small adjacent courtyard to create an effect of depth in which the wellhead forms the focal point.

1992

The floor of this, one of Venice's longest-established hotels, was inspired by the marble claddings of the city's churches and confraternities. The architects Carlo Aymonino and Gabriella Barbini have created a collection of characteristic perspective effects that add depth and give an illusion of greater space to the interior.

59 LABORATORIO ORSONI

1996
The gold and pearl-grey glass paste tesserae that cover the floor of the administration and reception area of Angelo Orsoni's company have been arranged in accordance with a precise design contrived by the artist of the family, Luca Orsoni, who is also the creator of the multicoloured wall panel.

Like a long torrential river, the decorative pattern of the floor goes beyond the confines of the room, extending longitudinally through three rooms and ascending seamlessly up the massive wooden doors.

following pages
Loggia of Palazzo Ducale. The light terrazzo floors in stucco, lime and marble chips adapt to the flowing rhythms of the broad arches, reflecting the shimmering light from the water that filters through the tracery of the mullioned apertures.

HISTORICAL NOTES

1 ST MARK'S BASILICA

9th–16th century

Floor in opus sectile *and* opus tessellatum

Piazza San Marco

"San Marco, the church, did not present itself to me simply as a monument but as the destination at the end of a boat trip across the sea in springtime, the basilica itself forming a living, indivisible whole with the waters. My mother and I went into the baptistery, both treading the marble and glass mosaic of the floor." That was how Marcel Proust felt in *La Fugitive* on stepping into St Mark's Basilica. It is still possible today to stand on the 2098.8 square metres of precious tesserae, the glittering colours of which are so evocatively rich in symbolism. The patterns in *opus sectile*, which identify the various functions of the interior spaces, probably date back to the third church, completed by Doge Domenico Contarini, who called it the Doges' Chapel, in 1071, the date inscribed on the memorial plaque set in the narthex by Francesco Sansovino towards the end of the sixteenth century. From the eleventh to the twelfth century, the first to work on St Mark's were artisans from the East, who brought with them their techniques and models. Then it was the turn of craftsmen from Ravenna and finally local workers. The *opus sectile* technique, already described in detail by Vitruvius and Pliny the Elder, is a very costly procedure, not only because of the valuable materials required, but also because of its difficulty of execution. Materials of particular hardness, strength, structure and thickness, such as serpentine porphyry, chalcedony, lapis lazuli and malachite, are selected and carefully cut by highly specialized artisans to obtain the segments necessary to create the precise geometrical shapes into which will subsequently be inserted small panels in *opus tessellatum* (mosaic). It is these unique figurative elements, which are relatively fragile and have to be replaced over time, that reflect the tastes and techniques of successive re-elaborations, some of which have even modified the iconography. In the central nave, slabs of Proconnesus marble, framed by a pattern of diamond-shaped and circular designs, cover the area lit by the three domes. The aisles are decorated with a continuous ribbon enclosing symmetrical octagons made up of small triangles. The sacred character of what was the Doges' Chapel is underlined by the lavish use of porphyry, a stone that, for the Byzantine emperors, symbolized immortality.

2 CHURCH OF SANT'ILARIO

9th century; destroyed

Mosaic floor from the same period

Fragments on display in the courtyard of the Procuratie Nuove in Piazza San Marco

Historical sources tell us that the abbey of Sant'Ilario was founded in 818 or 819 by Benedictine monks from the island of San Servolo, thanks to a donation by Doge Angelo Partecipazio. The building had the plan of a basilica, with a nave, two aisles and no transept. It was abandoned in the thirteenth century because of a dispute with the city of Padua, the effluents from which continued to flood the area. Four fragments discovered during excavations carried out in 1873–85 enable the mosaic floor to be dated to the ninth century. They are, however, insufficient to reconstruct the design, which must have resembled that in the church at Gazzo Veronese, albeit with more sophisticated decoration.

3 CHURCH OF SAN LORENZO

1592–1617, Simone Sorella
*12th-century mosaic floor recovered
during excavations carried out by the Venice
Soprintendenza ai beni ambientali e
architettonici.*
Castello, campo San Lorenzo

Sansovino describes the origins of San Lorenzo thus: "When Angelo Partecipazio was doge in 809, he built San Lorenzo and San Severo on the islands called Gemelle, or The Twins, and gave them to the monks to live in. But Orso, son of Giovanni, the Eleventh Doge and grandson of Angelo, installed nuns there in 841 when he was bishop of Olivolo, appointing his sister, Romana, abbess. He left in his will the church of San Severo ... and all the surrounding properties to the Benedictine nuns from noble families." The church was richly decorated and had many relics and tombs, including under the portico that of *Marco Polo known as Milione*. After various transformations, it appears today as it did in 1592, when Simone Sorella left the façade unfinished. Inside, a sumptuous altar by Gerolamo Campagna divides the church into two sections, one for the nuns, who belonged to an enclosed order, and the other for the congregation. San Lorenzo was stripped of its treasures at the time of the suppression of religious orders under Napoleon and was further damaged during the First World War. Structural restoration began only recently, but it was thanks to that work that in 1987, at a depth of 175 cm, a number of fragments of *opus sectile* and *opus tessellatum* were found. One particularly interesting fragment, which bears inscriptions, is located between two series of arches, which indicates that the floor was reconstructed. Given the stylistic and thematic motifs of the decoration and elaboration, which are very similar to those in St Mark's, San Zaccaria and San Donato, the floor is datable to the second half of the twelfth century. Today, the mosaic floor still covers – it is not known to what extent – the floor, in red Verona stone and Istrian stone, of the central nave and the presbytery of the earlier church.

4 CHURCH OF SANTI MARIA E DONATO AT MURANO

12th century
Floor dating from 1141 in mosaic, opus sectile
and opus vermiculatum *restored in 1973–79
by the Save Venice committee and by the
Venice Soprintendenza ai beni ambientali e
architettonici*
Murano, fondamenta Giustiniani

"At Murano, every fragment is variegated, and all are arranged with a skill and feeling not to be taught, and to be observed with great reverence, for that pavement is not dateless, like the rest of the church." Ruskin's eulogy of the mosaic floor at San Donato does not end here, for he goes on to affirm that the church is not only one of Italy's most precious monuments, but also that its floor contains the roots of the Venetian use of colour that would flower in the work of Titian. The church, dedicated first to St Mary and then to St Donatus, is the only one in the lagoon that conserves its Romanesque character intact. It is also the only one that still boasts the original composition of the floor, which dates back to 1141. The date is written in the centre of the mosaic floor covering the first half of the nave. Its rectangular pattern measures 6.95 x 7.22 metres and contains five circles with concentric elements. Four of these, with a diameter of 3.2 metres, are located in the corners. A smaller circle, measuring 2.2 metres across, lies in the centre. The interstices between the circles are decorated on each side by two pairs of peacocks, symbols of immortality, pecking corn, the nourishment of both body and soul, from a cup that represents abundance. The vertically positioned figures are griffins in heraldic positions. The four scenes deteriorated and have been restored. The strategic position of the entire composition emphasizes its symbolic value. The series of concentric circles represents the heavens and the rectangle represents the earth, the terrestrial paradise. Five rectangular slabs of marble form a sort of antechamber. They are finely carved on the back, which leads us to suppose they were recycled late classical gravestones, a discovery made during a major restoration project that went on for six years (1973–79). Financed by Gladys Del Mas of the American Save Venice committee, chaired by John McAndrew, and carried out under the supervision of the Venice Soprintendenza ai beni ambientali e architettonici (Environmental and Architectural Heritage Office), the restoration programme was an exemplary – and unique – rescue operation. Deterioration was at an advanced stage because of wear and tear, erosion, subsidence and above all the destructive effects of high tides, so radical intervention was required. The entire floor was removed (500 square metres in the central nave alone), an isolation tank was set up, and each marble tessera was individually cleaned before being put back in place according to the original design. The project was executed by the Zerbo e Francalanci company (the mosaicists were Diego Malvestio and his assistants). It was an enormous task, but this was the only procedure that could guarantee the recovery of this supremely beautiful work, even if the results of the restoration risk being undermined without an ongoing programme of maintenance.

5 CHURCH OF SAN ZACCARIA

12th century

Chapel of San Tarasio: mosaic floor dating from 1176

Castello, campo San Zaccaria

The church was founded in the ninth century during the rule of Doge Giustiniano Partecipazio (827–829), whose will included substantial bequests to the Benedictine nuns in the attached convent. The monastic institution was further enriched in the tenth and eleventh centuries by donations of property on the mainland and became one of the most socially prestigious establishments in the city. It was under the direct protection of the doge, who came to visit every year, and was the place where the Venetian aristocracy sent its daughters to be educated. Little is known about the church. Indirect sources suggest that it was damaged by a fire that swept the city in 1105, for an inscription dated 1176 mentions work that was carried out at that time. The mosaic decorations discovered on the floor in the main apse and part of the choir – today the chapel of San Tarasio – are probably also to be attributed to the same period, since the naturalism with which the animals are depicted is highly reminiscent both of the fourth-century floors in Aquileia and of the ones found at Skhira (Sfax) in Tunisia.

6 BASILICA OF SANTA MARIA ASSUNTA AT TORCELLO

9th–11th century

Floor dating from the 9th and the second half of the 12th century in opus sectile *and* opus tessellatum

Torcello

The church is a ninth-century Veneto-Byzantine building to the plan of a basilica with a nave, two aisles and a raised choir. The floor is almost entirely in marble and *opus sectile,* with a few elements in *opus tessellatum.* The absence of figurative motifs is striking. The overall design is laid out to a precise pattern that highlights the various parts of the church. The most interesting of these – and unique in Venice – is the floor of the central nave in front of the iconostasis, which draws on Arab and Sicilian floors from the Romanesque period. This insertion, and the references, particularly in the choir, to elements already present at St Mark's and San Donato, suggests that the Torcello floor is the least ancient of the three and should be dated to around the sixth or seventh decade of the twelfth century. Two fragments of an earlier floor were found in 1940 at a depth of 22 cm below the present one. The cushioned composition in the sixth intercolumnar space of the right-hand aisle is in black on a white background and features cut circles and octagons. The tesserae are laid in a rare, oblique, overlapping pattern, similar to that in Sant'Ilario. It was installed in the ninth century and is probably the earliest church floor still in place. Unfortunately, it has not been possible to make a detailed study, as this would involve the removal of the later floor on top.

7 CAMPO DELLA MADONNA DELL'ORTO

Paving dating from the second half of the 14th century in herring-bone-pattern brick and bands of Istrian stone

Cannaregio

This paving is reminiscent of the one that covered Piazza San Marco from 1264 to 1723 and can be seen in the *Procession of the Cross in the Piazza San Marco,* painted by Gentile Bellini at the end of the fifteenth century. It featured brick paving in a herring-bone pattern inserted into intersecting bands of Istrian stone to form continuous squares. A central aisle, again in Istrian stone, led from the main entrance of the church to the canal opposite.

8 PALAZZO GIUSTINIAN BRANDOLINI

Mid–15th century; attributed to Bartolomeo Bon

Courtyard: paving from the same period in herring-bone-pattern brick and bands of Istrian stone

Dorsoduro (private: visitors not admitted)

Part of a complex formed by two buildings with the same name, Palazzo Giustinian overlooks the Grand Canal in a line with Ca' Foscari, the building on the corner facing on to the nearby Rio Nuovo, built where the third Palazzo Giustinian used to stand. The buildings can be dated to the middle of the fifteenth century and are probably by Bartolomeo Bon, although they have been much restructured. They are a superb example of typically Venetian twin palazzi from the floral Gothic period. Erected symmetrically, they are linked by a wall with a main central gate and a series of three windows set one above the other for each storey. The main gate actually leads to a passageway through to the calle, or street, which was once private. The two lateral entrances take the visitor into the respective palazzi, the first of which still has the original paving in the courtyard and an ancient well. The internal façade was renovated in the sixteenth century. In 1858 Richard Wagner lived here for seven months while he was writing the final version of his opera *Tristan und Isolde.*

9 CHURCH OF SANTA MARIA DEI MIRACOLI

1481–94, Pietro Lombardo and workshop

Floor from the same period in marble inserts

Cannaregio, campo dei Miracoli

The church was built in 1481–94 by Pietro Lombardo with the assistance of his sons and the many *tajapiera*, or highly skilled artistic stonemasons, who worked at his workshop, and is lined throughout in precious marble of various kinds. Although distinctly Venetian in conception – compare Ca' d'Oro and Carpaccio's vast *teleri* paintings – the mouldings on the façade and the raised presbytery of this early Renaissance masterpiece recall the church of San Miniato in Florence. Santa Maria dei Miracoli was erected by popular demand on the spot where, on 26 January 1408, Francesco Amadi placed a miracle-working image of the Virgin Mary. It was the first church in Venice to be dedicated to the Immaculate Conception, thanks to the concession granted by Pope Sextus IV, who proclaimed the appropriate feast in 1476, although the dogma was not sanctioned until 1854. The building was praised at the time as the most beautiful church in the city after St Mark's, and as early as 1502 Sabellico rated it superior to all other places of worship for its construction and materials. The church was completely restored in 1987–97, thanks to the Save Venice committee, under the supervision of the Venice Soprintendenza ai beni ambientali e architettonici (director of operations: Mario Piana). Restoration work was carried out by the Ottorino Nonfarmale company (petrographic analyses by Lorenzo Lazzarini and Vasco Fassina).

10 SCUOLA TEDESCA

1528–29

Floor from the same period in terrazzo, restored in 1732–33

Cannaregio 2902 B, campo del Ghetto Nuovo

Site of the German Synagogue

The Scuole – which were places of collective devotion, guilds of arts and crafts, and communities of individuals of different faiths from different countries – played a major role in the social, economic and artistic fabric of the Republic of Venice. The synagogues belonged to this group of institutions. In Venice, there were five synagogues, the places of worship and assembly of the Jewish community. Three of them, the most ancient, stood around the campo del Ghetto Nuovo: the Scuola Tedesca, the Scuola al Canton and the Scuola Italiana. In observance of Jewish law, which demands that places of worship be built "in the high part of the city", in Venice, which is flat, they were located in the upper stories of unmarked buildings in the Ghetto, which were recognizable by their plain arched entrances and the large openings formed by five windows. For reasons of security, they were linked by long corridors and passageways. The oldest synagogue is the Scuola Tedesca. The plaque above the windows reads *when this edifice was erected, it was the year* 1528–9 *and it was rebuilt in* 1732–3. The structure is wedged in between the curve of the canal and the campo, or square, and it has the form of a quadrilateral. The anonymous architect who designed it has succeeded in lending harmony to the whole by placing a lantern in the centre. Originally, the *tevà* (pulpit) stood in the middle of the room under the lantern, and benches ran along the walls. Today, the pulpit has been moved to the wall facing the campo, obstructing two of the large windows, while the *aròn* (the cabinet where the Tables of the Law are kept), although it has been extended, still occupies its original position.

11 CHURCH OF SAN GIORGIO MAGGIORE

1566–1612, Andrea Palladio
Inlaid floor from 1591–96.
Outside paving from 1678–83 in trachyte and Istrian stone
Island of San Giorgio

The church of San Giorgio Maggiore, together with the adjoining Benedictine monastery, is one of Venice's most emblematic landmarks. Strategically positioned in the middle of the Bacino di San Marco, San Giorgio Maggiore was also significant because of its close cultural and political links with the centres of power in the city. Construction of the church began on 3 March 1566 under Abbot Andrea Pampuro from Asolo, but was finished only after Palladio's death. Abbot Michele Alabardi therefore had to complete the decoration of the interior in 1591–96, adding altars, columns, the choir and flooring. As in many Venetian churches, especially those in the Palladian idiom, the structure is rigorous and the spaces are laid out in precise geometrical relationships that are highlighted by the white stucco. The only note of colour is provided by the floors, which reflect the warm light that floods in through the great windows.

12 MONASTERY OF SAN GIORGIO MAGGIORE

Grand staircase: 1644, Baldassare Longhena
Floor from the same period in coloured marble
Island of San Giorgio
Giorgio Cini Foundation

"Longhena created a staircase with two flights and superimposed galleries. It is the most theatrical of all the staircases he executed and the most sumptuous in the city, where by tradition unprepossessing staircases were built even in important edifices. This magnificent structure attracted keen interest but had no imitators." These words, by Elena Bassi, confirm that this is the most prestigious monumental staircase in Venice because of both its spectacular visual impact and its dimensions. Only in the Baroque period would it have been possible to occupy such a large space with a staircase, although as early as 1579 Palladio had envisaged a monumental structure. The enlargement of space and the perspective effects are emphasized by the coloured patterns of the landings and the floor in various kinds of precious marble, laid out to a design by Longhena, although this is not documented. The date of construction (1644) is inscribed on the architrave above the niche of the central landing.

13 CHURCH OF THE REDENTORE

1577–92, Andrea Palladio
Apse: floor from 1616 in coloured marble
to a design probably by Palladio
Giudecca, fondamenta San Giacomo

The Redentore is one of the few designs by Andrea Palladio to have been executed exactly as he originally conceived it. In addition, the Venetian Senate promulgated a decree that allowed the Capuchins to ban the location of tombs inside the church because masses celebrated for the dead, bequests and legacies would have generated a substantial income that was incompatible with their vow of poverty. This preserved the purity and harmony of the edifice, which remained uncontaminated by the lavish and often pretentious funerary monuments of the kind erected in other places of worship. The first stone was laid by Doge Alvise Mocenigo on 3 May 1577, but work was completed only under proto (supervisor) Antonio da Ponte and his assistants in 1592, fully twelve years after Palladio's death. The various sections of the church – central nave, aisles, side chapels, the dome-crowned presbytery and choir – are picked out and melded together by curved elements. The entire plan, in its rigorous shades of white and grey, is illuminated by light reflecting off the floor, which thus becomes a further instrument by which to identify the spaces. The nave is in white and red and the presbytery, the semicircles of which were reserved for dignitaries, is in precious marble with shades of grey, black and white inserted in pink elements. The date 1616, which refers to the completion of the floor, is inscribed on the column on the right-hand side of the presbytery.

14 CHURCH OF SAN SALVADOR

1507–34, Giorgio Spavento, Tullio
Lombardo and Jacopo Sansovino
Floor from second half of 17th century
in coloured marble
San Marco, Mercerie di San Salvador

This church is situated at the beginning of the Mercerie, the main thoroughfare between St Mark's and Rialto. It is a very ancient foundation, perhaps dating from as long ago as the seventh century. It was restructured in the twelfth century and totally rebuilt after 1507, initially by Giorgio Spavento, then by Tullio Lombardo, before being finally completed by Jacopo Sansovino in 1534. Laid out to a Latin-cross plan, San Salvador was begun one year after the first stone for St Peter's in the Vatican had been laid and may be considered the masterpiece of the Venetian High Renaissance, second in importance only to St Mark's. It was founded by the Canons Regular of St Augustine, who were often suspected of heresy because of their independence of spirit in resisting the centralizing tendencies of Rome, and was a political response on the part of Venice's republican religious faith to the supremacy of the papacy of Julius II. San Salvador is the burial place of the rich Venetian merchants whose shops stood along the Mercerie. Thanks to the epigraphs on their tombs, it is possible to date the coloured marble floor, a Baroque addition that nevertheless reflects the spatial rigour of the building since it is based on precise modules derived from the mathematical theories of Luca Pacioli. The oldest surviving inscription, in Latin, is situated in the corners of the square containing the projection of the central dome. It commemorates the donor, a merchant named Tasca who died at the age of 63 in 1641. Pasquale Cicogna mentions other inscriptions that are no longer extant or have become illegible, such as the one that records *Piero Gerolamo and Bortolo Q. pistori* [dairymen] *and their heirs in the year* 1653, *Bortolo Batochi, merchant of Cretan wines, in the year* 1664.

15 MONASTERY OF SAN DOMENICO

1664–66, Baldassare Longhena

Grand staircase: inlaid floor from the same period attributed to Longhena and completed by Antonio Bonini

Castello, campo San Giovanni e Paolo

Administrative offices of the Public Hospital

In 1664–66 Baldassare Longhena built the monumental staircase of the monastery of San Domenico at San Giovanni e Paolo, creating a half-scale variation of the grand staircase at San Giorgio. The landing floors are particularly interesting and have been described by Elena Bassi in the following terms: "adorned by bright carpets of marble incrustations with floral motifs, they were laid by the Venetian artist Antonio Bonini in 1666." It is a true masterpiece, worthy of the finest workshop of the hard stones that were so popular from the Baroque period onwards. San Domenico is the first example in Venice of a Florentine, or inlaid, floor, and it was Baldassare Longhena who had it installed. Elena Bassi tells us that Longhena, as well as being the architect of the church of Santa Maria della Salute, also designed the floor in its presbytery and the central rose window. Unfortunately, there are no indications that he designed the landings for this staircase, which are, however, very fine indeed. The floor of the first landing, in fine condition, is inlaid, whereas in that on the ground, which has suffered some damage, probably from humidity, a number of ruined marble elements have been replaced by marble chips and mosaic tesserae in the same material inserted into the plug, a technique more suited to Venetian craftsmen.

16 BASILICA OF SANTA MARIA DELLA SALUTE

1631–87, Baldassare Longhena

Floor from the same period with inlays to a design by Longhena

Outside paving in trachyte and Istrian stone

Dorsoduro, campo della Salute

The commission for Santa Maria della Salute was awarded to Baldassare Longhena in 1630 by the Venetian Senate in compliance with a decree that the Republic would build a votive church to the Virgin if the city were saved from the plague. The building stands on Venice's main waterway at the top of an unusually imposing flight of stairs, and is the Baroque emblem to Venetian pietàs and the independence of the Most Serene Republic from the temporal power of the Church at a time of political uncertainty. Longhena described his project thus: "Since the church has the mystery of its dedication, being erected to the name of the Blessed Virgin, it seemed to me right, in the light of what little virtue the Good Lord has lent me, to construct it to a round plan, so that it should have the form of a crown to be dedicated to the Virgin." The floor decoration has great importance in the overall project for the edifice, as is confirmed by the ink sketch conserved in the Museo Correr, in which Longhena himself drew the motif and the measurements of both the presbytery floor and the rosette under the lantern. The floor is thus the key to any reading of the building from both the symbolic and the structural points of view.

17 CA' ZENOBIO

1684–1700, Antonio Gaspari

Floor from the same period in coloured marble to a design by Gaspari

Dorsoduro 2593–2597

Armenian College

A striking design by Antonio Gaspari for the recently ennobled and seriously rich Zenobio family, this markedly 'Roman' palazzo was constructed on a medieval, or perhaps fourteenth-century, building that had previously belonged to the Morosinis. This is a Venetian example of a Roman-style façade in which the central part, corresponding to a T-shaped portico on the plan, is highlighted by three balconies and the great Serlian, or Venetian, window of the main hall, surmounted by a curved tympanum decorated with an elaborate coat of arms. The extensions of the two wings of the internal façade looking on to the garden are in the manner of Borromini. The stylistic harmony of the palazzo is also manifest in the painted decoration. The ceiling of the superb ballroom was commissioned in 1688 from an artist of the Roman school, Louis Dorigny, while Ceres and Bacchus are the classical subjects of another ceiling painted by Gregorio Lazzarini in 1700. We have no certain proof of who created the design for the flooring of the main staircase, for there are many drawings by both Longhena and Gaspari. It may, however, reasonably be considered the work of the latter, partly because of the wealth of details relating to the palazzo, and because of the precise, pertinent design of the landings that mark off and lend prominence to the spaces of the staircase. As is shown by documents conserved at the Museo Correr, Gaspari – a pupil of Longhena who completed the projects his master left unfinished – did not restrict himself to drawing up the architectural plans for his building projects.

18 PALAZZO CONDULMER

Early 18th century
Terrazzo floor from the same period
restored by Roberto Crovato in 1982
Santa Croce (private: visitors not admitted)

The aristocratic Condulmer family – whose scions include Pope Eugenius IV, who died in 1447 – is mentioned by Giuseppe Tassini as owning a palazzo at the Tolentini, which had previously belonged to the Loredan family. It was here that, "on 8 August 1743, the feast of San Gaetano, the nobleman Condulmer invited the family of the Duke of Modena to enjoy the celebrations. There was a fine reception, illuminations in the garden and a courtly serenade, all at the expense of Condulmer, who was a celebrated gambler and had won large sums of money from the crown princess." There are no reliable sources for the date of the floor, but the technique of its execution and the stylistic characteristics of the building – which Lorenzetti dates to the eighteenth century – make it probable that it was completed in the early years of the eighteenth century. It is one of the city's finest and most ornate floors for the intricacy of its design, as well as for the precious materials used, and is without doubt the work of a major artist.

19 CHURCH OF SAN NICOLÒ DA TOLENTINO

1591–1602, Vincenzo Scamozzi
1706–14, Andrea Tirali
Late 16th-century floor in coloured marble.
Outside paving from 1706–14 to a design
by Tirali
Santa Croce, campo dei Tolentini

The Theatine order fled from Rome after the sack of 1527 and founded an oratory in Venice the following year. In 1591 the order commissioned Vincenzo Scamozzi, then the leading architect in Venice, to design a church. Work had already begun when Scamozzi was removed from the project, and building continued under the direction of a member of the order. The building was consecrated in 1602 despite being incomplete, and, in 1706–14, Andrea Tirali erected the pronaos, or free-standing portico, in front of the façade and the balustrade on the canal bank opposite, both probably to designs by Scamozzi. In 1731 Tirali, the proto, or supervisor, of the monasteries, extended the monastery in compliance with Venetian tradition, allowing us to appreciate what the proportions of the building would have been if it had been completed according to the earlier design by Andrea Palladio. There were many interventions by other architects: for example the two floors of the altars are in the Palladian idiom and date from the period when Scamozzi was at work. In contrast, the pronaos floor is by Tirali, whose design echoes the stucco elements in the vault, and who, after softening the Neo-classical rigour of its motifs with curved lines, used it as a link between the projection of the staircase, the small square opposite, and the balustrade on the canal, achieving a combination of perspectives that gives great breadth to the façade and to the volume of the church.

20 CA' PESARO

1652–82, Baldassare Longhena
1703–10, Antonio Gaspari
*Floor from 1710 with inlays to a design
by Gaspari*
Santa Croce 2076, fondamenta Pesaro
Museum of Modern Art

Although the contribution of Baldassare Longhena to the construction of the current building is not documented, the attribution is based on other projects that the architect carried out for the Pesaro family, such as the funerary monument of Doge Giovanni Pesaro in the church of the Frari, completed in 1669. The design here involved the unification of three separate adjacent buildings to create one of the largest palazzi in Venice. Work was begun in 1628 on the side overlooking the Grand Canal, by Longhena, who was commissioned by Procuratore Leonardo Pesaro, but only got under way seriously around 1663. In 1682, on the death of both the principal and his architect, work stopped at the first floor, as may be seen from the print by Luca Carlevarijs of 1703. The heirs subsequently entrusted completion of the palazzo to Antonio Gaspari, who finished his appointed task briskly. Indeed, it can be seen from the plan by Coronelli dated 1710 that building work had been concluded. The Museo Correr conserves thirty-three drawings of Ca' Pesaro by both Longhena and Gaspari. In one of these, by Longhena, the main staircase is located in the middle of the passageway. In the end, Gaspari found a more satisfying solution in placing it in a square-plan area to the side so as not to compromise the continuity of the line formed by the canal, the passageway and the courtyard.

21 PALAZZO TREVISAN MORO

Late 16th century
Terrazzo floor from the early 18th century
Cannaregio (private: visitors not admitted)

Situated in the Ghetto Nuovissimo at the junction of the Ghetto Nuovo and San Gerolamo canals, this building comprises two five-storey palazzi, each in three sections. Attributed to Jacopo Sansovino, who worked on the nearby Palazzo Moro, the building originally featured two pairs of apartments, one above the other, each lodging comprising a piano nobile, or main floor, half of the ground floor and another floor, either the mezzanine or the attic. The apartments were arranged around rooms on each floor that ran from the street to the canal, and were divided in half on the ground floor in correspondence with the four main gates on to the canal. The painted surfaces on the façade and the height of the openings on the main floors confer on the palazzo the appearance of opulence that at the end of the sixteenth century distinguished the great rented houses. Foreign residents in Venice could not purchase houses but only rent them, and the activities of the Jewish community included, in addition to money-lending, hiring out furniture and ornaments for such properties. The edifice is known today as Palazzo Da Silva because in 1584 it was the residence of Gusman Da Silva, Duke of Medina Sidonia, who was commissioned by King Philip II of Spain to acquire books in Venice for the new library of the Escorial. In Thomas Coryat's *Crudities*, we learn that Sir Henry Wotton, the first English ambassador resident in the city, who was a scholar, an authority on Palladio and a friend of Paolo Sarpi, lived here in 1605–11 during the first of his three tours of duty in Venice. One of his guests was the Anglican theologian William Bedell, who, during the papal interdict of Paul V, allowed Venetians to attend his services, where they could obtain copies of the Bible in Diodati's translation. It appears that Wotton also saved Coryat from the wrath of the Jews in the nearby Ghetto. After the Ghetto Nuovissimo was created in 1663, this was the only palazzo that stood within its bounds. It was acquired in the early years of the eighteenth century by the Treves family, one of the richest Jewish families in Venice. Their descendants still possess the plan and the furniture of the library, the floor of which is a rare example of the *chinoiserie* motifs so popular in the city during the eighteenth century.

22 PALAZZO PISANI AT SANTO STEFANO

1614–15, 1728–30, Bartolomeo Monopol and Girolamo Frigimelica

Terrazzo floor from the early 18th century

San Marco 3395, campiello Pisani

Ca' Pisani Nova, as indicated in the drawing from Canaletto's sketchpad conserved in the Accademia, is one of Venice's most prestigious palazzi. This was how Martinoni described it in his 1663 additions to the *Venezia città nobilissima ...* of Francesco Sansovino: "At Santo Stefano stands the marvellous palazzo of the brothers Luigi and Almorò Pisani, both Procuratori di San Marco. Superbly built after the Roman manner at great expense, it is rich in marble and beautiful carvings, with loggias, courtyards and other ornaments." The palazzo was built in several stages, with a first section dating from 1614–15, but it was damaged in the earthquake of 1637 and completed in its present form by Girolamo Frigimelica, who was also responsible for Villa Pisani at Stra. Frigimelica was awarded the commission in 1728 and added the loggias and the second piano nobile, which were finished two years later, as can be seen from the drawings in Canaletto's sketchpad dated 1730.

23 CHURCH OF THE GESUITI

1715–28, Domenico Rossi

Floor from the same period with inlays to a design by Rossi

Apse and high altar: inlaid floor to a design by Giovanni Pozzo

Cannaregio, campo dei Gesuiti

Domenico Rossi's masterpiece stands on the site of an earlier building that belonged to the Crociferi ('Cross-bearers'), a religious order that was suppressed by Pope Alexander VII in 1656 because of its lax discipline. The Jesuits, who returned to Venice after being driven out to the popular cry of *andé in malora!* ('Go to hell!') at the time of the papal interdict in 1606, purchased the church and its convent in 1657, after obtaining, like the Jews, temporary permission to reside in Venice, to be renewed every three years. The Gesuiti is an outstanding example of the unity of architectural conception and lavishness of decoration and materials characteristic of the order, for the Jesuits wanted to make their presence felt in Venice by promoting a new aesthetic sensitivity. The longitudinal plan of the church with its inscribed transept opens out into deep side chapels with sumptuous altars by Giovanni Pozzo, who also designed the solomonic-columned high altar and the gold, green and black marble that decorates the stairs. The walls and columns are covered by white and green marble inlays, the soft folds of which also adorn the pulpit. White and gold stucco and brightly coloured frescoes shimmer in the vault. The façade, on which Giovanni Battista Fattoretto may have collaborated, was also once covered in coloured stucco.

24 CHURCH OF SAN MARCUOLA

1727–38, Giorgio Massari

Floor from the same period with inlays to a design by Massari

Cannaregio, campo San Marcuola

The history of the construction of San Marcuola, unfinished even today, is particularly complicated. The sources relate that Antonio Gaspari drew up at least four plans, none of which was executed, and that Giorgio Massari, who was commissioned in 1727 by the parish priest to direct reconstruction, received payment for his model only in 1738. Like Gaspari, Massari paid great attention to detail and finishing, selecting his assistants and artisans with care. All this makes it probable that the design for the church floor is also by Massari. The interior features a single nave and has an unusual layout, as the high altar is not in line with either of the two doors. However, the perspective effect created by the floor corrects this anomaly by an optical illusion.

25 CASIN DETTO DEL BAFFO

Early 18th century

Terrazzo floor from 1730

Giudecca (private: visitors not admitted)

Looking on to the Ponte Lungo canal in the middle of an unbroken row of buildings, Casin del Baffo is an unassuming two-storey house, the most remarkable feature of which is its pot-bellied wrought-iron balcony. According to an unwritten local tradition, it was the casino, or private club, of the satirical poet Giorgio Alvise Baffo (1694–1768). The owner, who shared the same surname (Nicolò Baffo), left it in his will to Anna Bacci, who was born here and in turn sold it to its current owner. When she died in the house in 1975, Anna Bacci was over one hundred years old. Giuseppe Tassini tells us that the Baffo family arrived in Venice from Parma in 827 and built the no-longer-extant church of San Secondo in Isola, and subsequently constructed the church of Santa Maria Maddalena in 1222 near their residence at Castel Baffo. Tassini relates that a young woman from the Baffo family who was carried off by the Turks in 1568 became the mother of Mehmet III and mentions Lodovico Baffo, captain of the Morosina galleass that fought with honour against the Ottomans at the victorious battle of Scio in 1667. According to Tassini, the family became extinct in 1768 on the death of Giorgio, the satirical, Venetian-dialect poet. But when he tells us that the family tomb was in the nearby church of San Giacomo, Tassini raises the suspicion that Nicolò might have been the poet's last descendant. On the second floor of the house there are three small rooms with terrazzo floors. The middle one, which opens on to a landing with a richly frescoed and stuccoed ceiling, has the date 1730 on the floor. The designs on the floor have a gambling theme and probably refer to the purpose for which the building was used.

26 SCUOLA GRANDE DEI CARMINI

1668–70, Baldassare Longhena

Floor from 1740 in coloured marble

Dorsoduro, campo Santa Margherita

The façades, designed by Baldassare Longhena in 1668–70, were executed unevenly probably because the architect's personal intervention was limited. The exterior is in fact a mélange of different architectural styles. The ashlar of the two lower orders on the side facing the calle and the monotonous series of windows are cold but more organically integrated and sober than the other prospect, with its double order of columns and Corinthian pilasters on very high plinths. The second side is also characterized by the uneven rhythm of its alternating tympana, although the irregularity of the architectural solutions might be justified by the need to adapt the façade to an existing building. The sumptuous interior decoration is much more successful. The superb stuccoes of the staircase are probably by Abbondio Stazio, while those in the upper rooms, executed in accordance with the directions of Longhena, appear to have been completed by Antonio Gaspari, who was working on the nearby Ca' Zenobio, after Longhena's death. The final touches were added to this lavish decoration in 1744, when Giambattista Tiepolo completed the frescoes.

27 PALAZZO BARBARIGO AT SANTA MARIA DEL GIGLIO

15th century

Terrazzo floor from 1707 and 1742 completed by Antonio Tessa and Bortolo Cecchin, respectively, to a design by Girolamo Mengozzi, known as Il Colonna

San Marco (private: visitors not admitted)

In 1707, on the occasion of the wedding of his son, Zuane Francesco, to Contarina Contarini, Gregorio Barbarigo undertook a series of restructuring interventions on the buildings overlooking the Grand Canal at Santa Maria del Giglio, which had belonged to the family since 1514. One of the operations was the repair of the red and white terrazzo floors in three rooms, as can be seen from a surviving invoice of the *terrazer* artisan Antonio Tessa – or Tes, or Tesa – dated 28 October 1707. In 1739, during a subsequent phase when Gregorio, son of Zuane Francesco, married Caterina Sagredo, "work began on the repair of the terrazzos" in the palazzo, a project entrusted to

Bortolo Cecchin, a *terrazer* who worked on the house, "Where reside the Most Illustrious and Excellent Noblemen Franco Barbarigo Father and Sons". The old floors were removed and the surface levelled, and by 1742 four rooms had already been already completed "in a design in paste" previously agreed with "Gregorio padron" and for which Cecchin declared himself forced to charge 22 lire per pace since he had paid for the glass paste, paints and the excellent artist. Moreover – Bortolo Cecchin claimed – the end result was even better than the drawings by the artist Girolamo Mengozzi, known as Il Colonna, whose name appears on bill 13 "for the terrazzo designs" of the mezzanine. It is in this part of the building, where Caterina moved in 1766 on the death of her husband Gregorio, that the most interesting floors are to be found. In the very year she was widowed, Caterina had a pierced heart added to the design of the terrazzo floor of her bedroom. The piano nobile of the palazzo, like the mezzanine, is richly decorated. The stuccoes by Carpoforo Mazzetti Tencalla, which are still intact, are set alongside Mengozzi's quadratura settings for frescoes by Giambattista Tiepolo. Pietro Longhi's series of paintings of game-shooting in the lagoon, which adorned the walls of the mezzanine, is now conserved in the Fondazione Scientifica Querini Stampalia.

28 PALAZZO PISANI MORETTA

About 1470

Floor from 1742–45: landings in coloured marble, rooms in terrazzo executed by the terrazeri, *Domenico and Giacomo Crovato, to a design by Francesco Zanchi.*

San Polo (private: visitors not admitted)

Built in the shape of a double C with a large courtyard to the south-west and protected by a high wall on the side facing the calle, the palazzo is a re-elaboration of an earlier Byzantine plan. The façade overlooking the Grand Canal has a double entrance and two main floors, a typical design that indicates the building was used by two families. In the eighteenth century the palazzo was completely restructured at the wish of Chiara Pisani. Work began on 9 August 1742 and progress is recorded in great detail in her account books, for this, like Palazzo Barbarigo at Santa Maria del Giglio, is one of the rare cases where there are numerous documents and records of payment that may be used to date the floors and identify with certainty the artists who designed and executed them. The proto who was in charge of restoration, which went on for three decades, was the artist Francesco Zanchi. It is to him that we owe the designs of the floors on the landings and the two piani nobili. The work was, however, carried out by Domenico and Giacomo Crovato, *terrazeri* and ancestors of the family that still keeps the ancient craft of laying terrazzo floors alive today in Venice.

29 PALAZZO TIEPOLO PAPADOPOLI

1560, Giangiacomo dei Grigi
Terrazzo floor from about 1745 to a design attributed to Giambattista Tiepolo and from 1874–75 by Michelangelo Guggenheim

San Polo (private: visitors not admitted)

The palazzo was built for the Coccina family about 1560 and has been attributed to Andrea Palladio, Alessandro Vittoria, Jacopo Sansovino as well as to Vincenzo Scamozzi, but it was in fact designed, as Lorenzetti correctly states, by Giangiacomo dei Grigi, the son and collaborator of the better-known Guglielmo, known as Il Bergamasco. The interior underwent radical alterations in 1874–75 under the direction of Michelangelo Guggenheim, to whom the Papadopoli family entrusted restoration work. In an article that appeared in the *Gazzetta di Venezia,* we read that "the sixteenth-century Palazzo Tiepolo has given birth to Palazzo Papadopoli in the nineteenth century".

30 PALAZZO CONTARINI AT SAN BENEDETTO

1560, attributed to Sante Lombardo
Terrazzo floor from about 1750
San Marco 3980, calle Contarini.
Compagnia Generale delle Acque building

The palazzo, attributed to Sante Lombardo, was probably built on an earlier Gothic edifice. In 1748, on the occasion of the wedding of Giulio Contarini to Eleonora Morosini, the interior was completely redecorated with frescoes by Francesco Fontebasso and Gasparo Diziani, sculptures by Giovan Maria Morlaiter and stuccoes by Carpoforo Mazzetti Tencalla and his pupils. The designs of the floors echo the stuccoes on the ceilings with such sophisticated elegance that we are tempted to conclude that they were executed, as was common practice at the time, by the same artists who decorated the walls and ceilings. In the main bedroom, there still survives a fine eighteenth-century wooden floor carved in a Rococo design. The outside courtyard is also noteworthy. Michelangelo Muraro wrote of it: "Having crossed the solemn portal that comprises the ground-floor entrance to Palazzo Contarini, one enters a 'noble and capacious courtyard' … separated from the surrounding streets by a high wall. In addition to the elegance of the loggia and the decoration of the walls, the geometrical pattern of the Istrian stone is brought out by the grey blocks of Euganean trachyte of the paving. The walls around it were decorated with frescoes by Fontebasso, depicting fountains and gods of the sea."

31 PALAZZO BARBARO

15th century
Terrazzo floor from about 1750
San Marco (private: visitors not admitted)

Palazzo Barbaro is an example of the ogival Mannerist architecture of the early fifteenth century. It is remarkable for the elegant decoration of the façade and the outside staircase that leads from the courtyard to the second floor. In 1694–98, Antonio Gaspari made radical alterations to the second floor of the building. Subsequently, in 1750, when Almorò Barbaro was elected Procuratore di San Marco, the palazzo was embellished with stuccoes and superb paintings, including the canvas by Giambattista Tiepolo, today in the Metropolitan Museum in New York, which celebrates his elevation on the ceiling of the dining-room. Palazzo Barbaro was the favourite Venetian residence of Henry James, who wrote here *The Wings of the Dove.*

32 PALAZZO SORANZO PIOVENE

Early 16th century, attributed to Sante Lombardo
Terrazzo floor from 1753
Courtyard: paving early 16th century in Euganean trachyte and Istrian stone attributed to Lombardo
Cannaregio 2174
Ispettorato Generale della Guardia di Finanza

The Piovene family, who originally came from Vicenza, was admitted to the Venetian aristocracy in 1655, when Antonio Piovene and his siblings paid 100,000 ducats to the state treasury. In 1670 Antonio's son, Girolamo, married Cecilia, daughter of Pietro Soranzo. Her dowry included this elegant palazzo, erected, probably by Sante Lombardo, during the Renaissance. The design of the paving that marks off the well in the courtyard also dates from the sixteenth century. Another Renaissance feature is the iron cable – the only one of its kind in Venice – that traverses the wall and was used to carry water up to the various floors of the building. In 1748–53 the palazzo underwent radical alterations, including the extension of the wing towards the garden, commissioned by Coriolan Piovene. It was Coriolan who decorated the walls of the entrance with four large paintings of the eighteenth-century Venetian school that celebrate the coronation of Dogaressa Zilia Dandolo, wife of Doge Lorenzo Priuli. Coriolan Piovene also had the other rooms decorated with stuccoes and frescoes on themes from mythology. The ones by Francesco Zugno in the Sala delle Allegorie are particularly outstanding. But the most remarkable feature of Palazzo Soranzo Piovene is the flooring. In the centre of the room overlooking the Grand Canal, there is – again, the only one of its kind in Venice – a perfectly executed terrazzo representation of a mythological subject that recalls the second- and third-century Roman mosaics from Cyprus and the North African coast.

33 CA' TRON

1570–80
Terrazzo floor from about 1772
Courtyard: paving from the same period as
interior in masegno and Istrian stone
Santa Croce 1957
Venice University Architectural Institute

Ca' Tron was restructured in the late sixteenth century and extended in the early eighteenth with the addition of two side wings and a huge ballroom that stood on the far side of the courtyard. Now demolished, the ballroom was probably the work of Antonio Gaspari, if we are to judge by its similarities to Ca' Zenobio. The corner room has an ornately decorated floor, the symbolic imagery of which reflects the personality of Caterina Dolfin. Caterina, who in 1772 married the elderly Procuratore Andrea Tron, was an educated woman (her nickname in Arcadia was Dorina Nonacrina). She was famous for the literary coterie she hosted as well as for her progressive ideas.

34 GALLERIE DELL'ACCADEMIA

15th century, Bartolomeo Bon
Floor from 1755–66 in coloured marble
to a design by Bernardino Maccaruzzi.
Dorsoduro 1050, campo della Carità

Built in 1206, the Scuola di Santa Maria della Carità, also known as the Scuola dei Battuti, or 'flagellants', is the most ancient of the six Scuole Grandi. This lay order of mutual charity and assistance to the poor has as its symbol a Greek cross set inside, and intertwining with, two circles. The Sala del Capitolo in this Gothic building still has the splendid wooden ceiling installed by the 'Guardian Grando', Ulisse Aliotti. Work on the ceiling went on from 1461 to 1484. Major alterations were made to the edifice between 1755 and 1766. The façade was restructured and a door inserted, while inside, a vestibule was added as well as the double staircase designed by Giorgio Massari and erected by his pupil, Bernardino Maccaruzzi. The staircase is embellished with two statues by Giovan Maria Morlaiter representing Faith and Charity. Despite the lack of documentary evidence, the design for the floor of the landings and main reception room can also be attributed to Maccaruzzi. Although the floors are of great artistic interest, they bear no relation to their general context, which forces us to conclude that they were not designed by Massari. The architect, who died before work was finished, was renowned for the care he took to ensure his interventions had an overall cohesion and were appropriate to their settings.

35 CASINO VENIER

18th century, attributed to
Bernardino Maccaruzzi
Floor from the same period with inlays
attributed to Maccaruzzi.
San Marco 4939, ponte dei Baretteri
Alliance Française

From the sixteenth century onwards, the casini, or private clubs, of Venice were 'places of delight' for amorous encounters, good conversation and gaming. Located on the Giudecca, in the countryside, on the mezzanine floors of the palazzi and above all in the district around Piazza San Marco, casini acquired a reputation during the eighteenth century for the social standing of their owners and guests as well as for the refined elegance of their furnishings. Despite the attempts of the State Inquisitors to have them closed down, there were still 136 of them when the Venetian Republic finally fell. Casino Venier is one of the best preserved of those that have survived to the present day. On map 427 of the Priuli land registry dated 14 February 1707, the Casino Venier is noted as belonging to Procuratore Federico Venier, and being at the disposal of his wife, Elena Priuli, a woman of culture and refinement. The property is also mentioned in a report, conserved in the archive of the Inquisitors, which claims that on 19 July 1792 the Inquisitors' spy, Marco Barbaro, saw a certain Messer Giacobi enter the building in the company of an actress and at the same time heard a number of male voices speaking French, when in theory aristocrats were not permitted to associate with non-Venetians. The Casino Venier is in a quiet location and can be recognized from the outside by its *liagò*, or belvedere, with the Venier crest, looking on to the Ponte dei Baretteri (literally the 'hatters' bridge') to keep an eye on business in the Mercerie. In the apparently unexceptional entrance, a side door opens to reveal a narrow stairway leading to the tiny apartments that still conserve their splendid eighteenth-century decorations. There are frescoed ceilings, stuccoed walls and mirrors with gratings so that guests could listen to the musicians without being seen, majolica stoves, marble floors with perspective designs and the ever-present peep-hole, jambs and the lower parts of the walls in pink Verona marble, and finally doors and fake cupboards in walnut and rosewood to conceal secret passages. The Casino Venier was restored by the French committee under the patronage of UNESCO, and since 1987 it has been the premises of the Alliance Française.

36 LIBRERIA MARCIANA

1537–54, Jacopo Sansovino
Floor in coloured marble: landings of staircase from 1559; anteroom and main hall from 1776 executed by Angelino Canciani and Francesco Bonazza for the Scuolo Grande della Misericordia
piazzetta San Marco
Biblioteca Nazionale Marciana

Francesco Sansovino in *Venetia Città Nobilissima …* describes the Libreria Marciana in the following terms: "On arriving at the palazzo, one sees the modern building called the Libreria. The first room is a public hall for lecturers paid by the Senate, who teach young people Greek and Latin letters. Here is conserved the Library of St Mark, as fine as any other in any part of Italy." The library was commissioned from Francesco's father, Jacopo, in 1536 to house the manuscripts donated by Francesco Petrarca and Cardinal Bessarion, as well as the library of Cardinal Hieronimo Leandro della Mota and Cardinal Grimani, which at the time were stored over the church of St Mark's. The superb staircase is resplendent in gold, carvings, stuccoes, marble and paintings that are the equal of those that decorate the Scala d'Oro in the Palazzo Ducale and whose present configuration we owe to Alessandro Vittoria, who worked on it from February 1559 to April 1560. Its two landings feature six composite Oriental marble columns that came from the dilapidated Basilica of Santa Maria in Cannedolo at Pula and were brought to Venice by Sansovino himself in 1541. The building was still incomplete in 1570, when Sansovino died, and was to undergo considerable alteration – which was not always successful – in subsequent years. The first of these interventions was by Vincenzo Scamozzi in the late sixteenth century, and they continued after the fall of the Republic when, in 1811, the Procuratie Nuove and the Libreria were restructured as a residence for the emperor of France and his viceroy.

37 PALAZZO LOREDAN AT SANTO STEFANO

First half of 16th century
Antonio Abbondi, known as Scarpagnino
Additions from first half of 17th century, Giovanni Grapiglia
Terrazzo floor from 1760 and 1807
San Marco 2945, campo Santo Stefano
Istituto Veneto di Scienze, Lettere e Arti

In 1536 the Loredan family, grandchildren of Doge Leonardo Loredan, who was superbly drawn by Gentile Bellini in the portrait that is now in the National Gallery in London, purchased a number of houses at San Vidal from Domenico Mocenigo. At the same time, they had them restructured "with modern architecture" – as Francesco Sansovino relates – probably by Antonio Abbondi, known as Scarpagnino. The elongated plaster façade facing on to the campo was, until the mid-seventeenth century, covered with frescoes of classical subjects by Giuseppe Salviati and Giallo Fiorentino. The wing, added in 1618 by Giovanni Grapiglia and wrongly attributed in the early nineteenth century to Andrea Palladio, has strong contrasts of light and shade and attractive proportions that derive from its marble cladding and the measured cadence of its columns. Inside, a spectacular staircase whose flights are decorated with arches and columns – probably by Scarpagnino – adds grace and vigour to the square hall, reached through two monumental symmetrical doors, one facing on to the canal and the other to the landward side. In the 1760s Francesco Loredan, who was in the final years of his rule as doge, had much of the piano nobile redecorated. Today, all that is left is one room overlooking the water and a small room sumptuously decorated with stuccoes by artists from the school of Abbondio Stazio. In 1806 Palazzo

Loredan became the residence of General Baraguay d'Hilliers, the first French governor of Venice, who in 1807 commissioned Giovanni Carlo Bevilacqua, a pupil of Canova, to paint a number of frescoes on Napoleonic themes. Naturally, these were destroyed when the Austrians returned in 1814. The floors, which look bare today without their frescoed ceilings, date from the same period.

38 PALAZZO VENDRAMIN AT THE CARMINI

Second half of 17th century
Terrazzo floor from 1770–75
Dorsoduro (private: visitors not admitted)

This is an unusually configured building, the main façade of which faces on to the gardens and kitchen garden to the rear. The secondary façade is formed by a courtyard protected by a wall, in which there is the main gate leading on to the fondamenta, or canal-side pavement, in front of the church of the Carmini. Palazzo Vendramin's Baroque style is clear from the high windows, which, together with their decoration, give it an uncompromisingly vertical thrust. A double entrance with marble bas-reliefs and stucco reminiscent of the work of Longhena links the staircase to the *pòrtego*, or portico, of the piano nobile. Stuccoes, frescoes and splendid terrazzo floors adorn all the rooms.

39 PALAZZO BONFADINI VIVANTE

Late 18th century
Terrazzo floor from 1776
Cannaregio 461
Azienda Multiservizi Ambientali Veneziana

A dignified, if externally unprepossessing, edifice with an elongated plan that was erected at the end of the eighteenth century to replace a group of unexceptional houses. Light reflecting off two canals illuminated its sumptuous interiors. The one running along the side of the palazzo has been filled in but the Cannaregio canal, on to which the main entrance in the façade opens, is still there. Restored in 1993 by the current owners, the Azienda Multiservizi Ambientali Veneziana, Palazzo Bonfadini Vivante still conserves its excellent stuccoes by Giuseppe Castelli, dating from towards the end of the eighteenth century. Castelli was also probably the artist, on stylistic grounds, who executed the elegant terrazzo floors on a white background. The walls and ceilings add volume to the rooms with their air-filled scenes and frescoed landscapes by Giovancarlo Bevilacqua, Giuseppe Borsato and Giovambattista Canal, as well as the moulded decorations by Castelli.

40 CASA ALBERTI

Late 16th century
Terrazzo floors from the second half of the 18th century, restored in 1998 by Giovanni Bortolazzo
Dorsoduro (private: visitors not admitted)

Tassini tells us that Gerolamo Alberti, who came from Florence, was granted Venetian citizenship in 1658 and in 1688 bought the houses at San Barnaba from Elisabetta Priuli, the widow of Leonardo Loredan. In 1711 Alberti declared to the Council of Ten that he owned the house where he lived as well as others in the neighbourhood, one of which had been unlet for some time "because the entertainment of boxing was no longer available". The Alberti family had 'Secretaries of State' who were resident abroad, of whom the most important was Francesco, an engineer and superintendent of the armoury at the time of the siege of Prague in 1657. His three sons rose to achieve high honours at the court of the Elector Palatine of the Rhine. This four-storey building looks on to the canal and the campo from a plain sixteenth-century façade with double Serlian windows and balconies that, like the matching entrances, highlight the presence of the double piano nobile. At the end of the eighteenth century the ceilings and walls of the piano nobile were stuccoed, and the terrazzo floors that echo their design were also relaid. The earliest of the floors, which is remarkable for the unusual rosette motif of the outer fascia, is located in the part of the sixteenth-century passage leading to the internal courtyard. In contrast, the floor of the corner room facing the canal, laid a few years later, is decorated with a central motif representing an island comprising an asymmetrically shaped garden over which a pelican is flying, a theme reminiscent of the floor from the same period in Palazzo Bonfadini.

41 PALAZZO MOCENIGO AT SAN SAMUELE
1570–90
Terrazzo floor from 1788
San Marco (private: visitors not admitted)

Vincenzo Maria Coronelli, a seventeenth-century Venetian cartographer, attributed this palazzo, which had not yet been finished in 1579, to Andrea Palladio. The actual architect was certainly a now-forgotten disciple of the great man. Giuseppe Filosi, in a print that enhances the building's impressive structure, depicted the arrival of guests to the sumptuous reception held in 1716 by Pisana Corner Mocenigo in honour of Frederick Augustus III of Denmark. In 1788, when Alvise Mocenigo was appointed Procuratore di San Marco, structural work on the various Mocenigo residences was carried out, including the ornate floor in the corner room. In 1818, Lord Byron lived here, and in a print of a slightly later date that portrays him at the palazzo we can recognize the floor that survives today.

42 PALAZZO MOCENIGO AT SAN STAE
Early 17th century
Terrazzo floor from 1787
Santa Croce 1992
Centro per lo Studio del Tessuto

The San Stae branch of the Mocenigo family was related to the San Samuele Mocenigos. This palazzo, which was already indicated in Jacopo de' Barbari's map of Venice in 1500, took its present form in the early seventeenth century when Alvise I, Provveditore, or governor, in Dalmatia, acquired the adjoining houses belonging to the Lando family to enlarge it. The floors, however, date from 1787, when another Alvise renovated the decorations with frescoes by Jacopo Guarana, Agostino Mengozzi, known as Il Colonna, and Giovan Antonio Zanetti. The palazzo was left to the city of Venice by the last descendant of the Mocenigo family, Alvise Nicolò, and is a fine example of an eighteenth-century patrician residence that has survived to the present day with its sumptuous furnishings intact.

43 HOUSE AT SANTO STEFANO
16th century
Terrazzo floor from about 1830, restored in 1975 by Francesco Crovato
San Marco (private: visitors not admitted)

In his *Itinéraire de Venise* of 1818, Giannantonio Moschini noted that the façade of this palazzo – once the property of the Barbaro family – still bore traces of the vast fresco of Sante Zago that blended in so beautifully with the scenery of Campo Santo Stefano opposite. Like the nearby Palazzo Cavalli Franchetti, this building, with its attractive asymmetrical Renaissance façade and two main doors framed in Istrian stone, belonged to the Cavalli family, as may be seen from the crest on the floor of the ground-floor entrance.

44 CAFFÈ FLORIAN
1858, Lodovico Cadorin
Floor from the same period in glass mosaic to a design probably by Cadorin
San Marco 56–59, Procuratie Nuove

In the eighteenth century, coffee-houses, of which there were twenty-six in Piazza San Marco alone, were not merely places to meet and gamble but also lively cultural centres. On 29 December 1720 Floriano Francesconi opened, under the Procuratie Nuove, La Venezia Trionfante, an establishment that was to become an institution in the city with the name of Caffè Florian. It was patronized by illustrious customers such as Jean-Jacques Rousseau, Francesco Guardi and Gasparo Gozzi, the last of whom used it as an office for his *Gazzetta Veneta*. In 1773, on Floriano's death, the business passed into the hands of his grandson Valentino, who took the coffee-house to even greater heights of fame. Its habitués included Ippolito Pindemonte and Ugo Foscolo; Antonio Canova and the satirical poet Pietro Buratti refreshed themselves here, as did the nationalist patriots Silvio Pellico, Daniele Manin and Niccolò Tommaseo; and on its hard sofas, John Ruskin rested between sketches of the capitals of the Palazzo Ducale. After a change of ownership, in 1857 the Caffè Florian assumed its present elegant appearance, thanks to the complete renovation carried out by Lodovico Cadorin. The flooring was relaid at that time and it is likely that the design customers can admire today is by the same architect. It was in this new Caffè Florian that visitors to the first Venice Biennale met in 1895. Later on, it was frequented by Marcel Proust, Sergej Diaghilev, Serge Lifar, Gabriele D'Annunzio, Eleonora Duse, Herman Melville, Tom Paine, Marchesa Casati and Contessa Morosini. The Caffè Florian remains today, as it always has been, a magical window on to the square through which to see and be seen.

45 PALAZZO CAVALLI FRANCHETTI
15th century, rebuilt in 1878–82 by Girolamo Manetti, Carlo Matscheg and Camillo Boito
Inlaid floor from the same period
San Marco 2847, campo San Vidal
Istituto Federale delle Casse di Risparmio

An outstanding example of floral Venetian fifteenth-century Gothic, Palazzo Cavalli Franchetti may be attributed, according to Giandomenico Romanelli, to the Roberti and Bon workshops which were active on both the Palazzo Ducale and Ca' d'Oro. On 9 February 1878 the building was sold by the Count of Chambord, who commissioned work from Giambattista Meduna, to Baron Franchetti, who would remain the owner until 1922. As soon as he had bought the property, Franchetti initiated an ambitious programme of alterations and restoration that he entrusted first to the engineer Gerolamo Manetti, and Carlo Matscheg from Belluno, before subsequently calling in Camillo Boito. It was Matscheg who in the 1880s completed work on the large entrance hall, and probably on the floor and tapered geometric elements on the ground floor as well.

46 CA' VENIER CONTARINI
16th–18th centuries
Terrazzo floor from 1892
San Marco (private: visitors not admitted)

Ca' Venier Contarini is a modestly proportioned palazzo facing on to the Grand Canal and features a Renaissance façade that has been grafted on to an earlier Gothic building, of which only the cornice remains. The volute-decorated lucarnes were added during the eighteenth century, and the interior was restructured in the nineteenth century, as is confirmed by the date inscribed on the staircase leading up to the second piano nobile. The floor in the main reception room on the second floor is especially interesting both for its design and because the material used is similar to that in one of the mezzanine floors at Palazzo Barbarigo.

47 PALAZZO CORNER CONTARINI CAVALLI
15th–17th centuries
Terrazzo floor from 1890, restored in 1983 by Roberto Crovato
San Marco 3978
Appeal Court

The building derives its name from the two horses depicted in the crest of the coats of arms on the façade, which has been much altered over the years. The ground floor, the mezzanine and the façade still reveal traces of the floral Gothic style and can be dated to around 1430, as can the ornate six-light central window. Other interventions took place at the end of the sixteenth century and in the early seventeenth, when the main branch of the Venier family moved to the palazzo at San Vidal. Further restoration work was carried out in the mid-eighteenth century, and it was then that the ceilings were frescoed, probably by Giacomo Guarana. About 1890 the interior was renovated and redecorated in the neo-Gothic manner. The elegant floor in what is today the presidency, which has been impeccably restructured by Antonio Foscari and Barbara Del Vicario, dates from that period.

48 BANCA COMMERCIALE ITALIANA

1875, Francesco Balduin

Terrazzo and inlaid floor from about 1893

San Marco 2188, via XXII marzo

After the fall of the Venetian Republic, the city's appearance underwent a number of profound changes. Thanks to highly skilled architects, artists and artisans, the fascination of rigorously scientific pastiche began to assert itself in the increasingly popular neo-Romanesque, neo-Gothic and neo-Renaissance styles. Venice was gripped in an iconoclastic fever. A decision dated 27 August 1875 transformed the San Moisè canal into what is today Calle Larga XXII Marzo, and the engineer Francesco Balduin drew up the plans for the new avenue with its buildings in the manner of Pietro Lombardo. One of the buildings Balduin designed was the Banca Commerciale Italiana, the Renaissance-inspired construction of which is typical of bourgeois Mannerism. It is noteworthy for its well-defined plan, its formal accuracy with respect to the classic canons of architecture, and the sumptuous materials used both for external decoration and in the interiors. The floors are among the finest of those laid at the time. They are superbly executed and richly ornamented in precious materials, offering ravishing combinations of colour and striking perspective effects that mirror and enhance the decoration of the walls and ceilings.

49 CA' D'ORO

1421–43, Matteo Raverti

Floor from 1896 in opus sectile *and* opus tessellatum

executed by Baron Giorgio Franchetti

Cannaregio 3933, calle della Ca' d'Oro

Galleria Franchetti

Ca' d'Oro, the most famous private building in Venice, was commissioned by Marino Contarini – a member of one of the most important families of the day – from Matteo Raverti, a stonemason, and Marco di Amadio, a *maestro di muro*, or 'wall mason'. It is one of the most remarkable examples of floral Gothic architecture from the first half of the fifteenth century. Despite the exalted status of its original owner, the palazzo was known as Ca' d'Oro, or the 'Golden House', even in the earliest surviving contemporary documents in which it is mentioned, because of its spectacularly extravagant appearance. The façade was a triumph of coloured marble, studded with round inlays in multi-coloured stone crowned by gilt balls. And in case this might have seemed over demure, in 1431 the artist Zuane de Franza (Jean Charlier) was given the task of highlighting the colours of the marble and stone, and picking out profiles and reliefs, in gold, vermilion, ultramarine and cerise. The effect can be seen today, at least in part, thanks to recent restoration work. At the end of the nineteenth century Ca' d'Oro was purchased by Baron Giorgio Franchetti to house his collections. Franchetti was an unusual patron of the arts. It was he who removed the neo-Gothic accretions that had been added around 1840 during the interventions by Giambattista Meduna for Prince Alexander Trubetskoi, who gave it to the dancer Maria Taglioni. Franchetti was so enraptured by the building that, inspired by the tarsias in St Mark's, he personally designed and executed the paving of the *pòrtego*, incorporating valuable coloured marble and ancient relics he had acquired from the most unlikely sources.

50 CASA ALLA SALUTE

1935, Fabrizio Clerici

Contemporary inlay, terrazzo and mosaic floor

executed by Antonio Crovato to a design by Clerici.

Dorsoduro (private: visitors not admitted)

The Casa alla Salute looks out on to the Grand Canal and the Giudecca opposite the volutes of Santa Maria della Salute. Its unassuming exterior encloses a number of elegant and unusual rooms in which the architect has employed traditional flooring techniques to delimit the functions of each space. The white and grey mosaic of the terrazza echoes the elaborate marble decoration of the walls of the church of the Gesuiti. The floors on the first storey are in terrazzo and in the main reception room, known as the Maggiotto room because of stucco-framed allegories of the twelve months, we find the same motif as in the bedroom of Palazzo Tiepolo Papadopoli. The ground-level floors are inlaid and terrazzo. Large Baroque gilt spires adorn the white marble in the entrance, while the dining-room, in the same marble, features a gilt, lapis lazuli-decorated star, a motif also present on the table-top.

51 HOTEL BAUER GRÜNWALD

1890, Giovanni Sardi
1938, Giovanni Berti
Terrazzo floor from 1938 executed by the Crovato brothers
San Marco 1458

In 1890 Giovanni Sardi designed a neo-Gothic edifice to house a hotel and a brewery that were well known at the time. The project involved the demolition of the Gothic Palazzo Manolesso-Ferro, built in the style of Pietro Lombardo, and a smaller adjoining palace. Subsequently, in 1938, the complex was raised and extended by Giovanni Berti, and in 1944–49 Sardi's sober façade looking on to Campo San Moisè and the canal of the same name was replaced by a travertine-clad prospect in a pseudo-Rationalist idiom that looks distinctly out of place in this architectural context. The seventeenth-century façade of the Scuola dei Fabbri has been incorporated into the façade, whereas the courtyard, the *calletta*, or alley, and the Barozzi bridge mysteriously disappeared one night in 1944.

52 HOTEL CIPRIANI

1956
Terrazzo floor from the same period decorated by Gerald Gallet
Giudecca 10

In 1956 Giuseppe Cipriani, the owner of Harry's Bar, revealed to his more discriminating customers an idea he had been nursing for some years – to build an exclusive hotel, far from the crush of tourists, that would still be only a few minutes away from Piazza San Marco. The wealthy, aristocratic Guinness family greeted the proposal with enthusiasm, so Cipriani set to work, having selected a suitable location at one end of the Giudecca with a view towards St Mark's. It is in the area facing the gardens of the Zitelle, on the former site of the Camaldolite monastery of San Giovanni Battista, which was suppressed in 1767. Tradition has it that the Zitelle, or 'spinsters', took its name from the closed-order convent for the daughters of noble Venetian families that used to stand there. Even today, the hotel is set in the Orti di Casanova, or 'Casanova's gardens', which take their name from the great seducer, who at night would come to visit the young women shut up in the convent. The hotel itself is a long building with a low profile hidden in the greenery, with views on to the swimming pool, the island of San Giorgio and the lagoon.

53 SHOP AT PIAZZA SAN MARCO

1957–58, Carlo Scarpa
Mosaic floor from the same period to a design by Scarpa, in collaboration with Carlo Maschietto, executed by Antonio Crovato.
San Marco 101, Procuratie Vecchie

Only in Venice, where beauty is truly sublime and ugliness often execrable, could the former Olivetti shop stand in the very heart of the city – Piazza San Marco – as if had always been there. And only a true Venetian, with the sensitivity of Carlo Scarpa, could have transformed a derelict site backing on to what resembled an unlit urinal into an exclusive viewpoint on to the loveliest square in the world. The continuity of interior and exterior, highlighted by slender partitions, multiplies volumes and perspectives, creating an ever-changing parade of images and emotions. The glass-paste mosaic floor reflects the light that floods in through the generous windows, further enhancing the overall effect.

54 FONDAZIONE SCIENTIFICA QUERINI STAMPALIA
1961–63, Carlo Scarpa
Mosaic flooring from the same period to a design by Scarpa, in collaboration with Carlo Maschietto, executed by Luciano Zennaro.
Castello 4778, campo Querini Stampalia

Carlo Scarpa's intervention has enabled the ground floor to be used again, enhancing the palazzo's canalside prospect. Large apertures allow both light and water to enter freely, creating a symmetrical balance with the garden to the rear. Flights of steps and walkways lend movement to the passage. Access is over a beautifully ornamented bridge constructed from carefully selected materials in the Japanese style. Slanting stairways lead to the tiny entrance, which is brightened by flooring made from small coloured squares of marble. The design was inspired by the space research of Scarpa's friend Mario De Luigi, and the entrance is surrounded along the perimeter walls by a gutter in Istrian stone that allows water to flow in and out.

55 PALAZZO REMER
Early 15th century, restructured in 1985–86 by Paolo Piva
Flooring from 1986 designed by Paolo Piva
Cannaregio (private: visitors not admitted)

The main façade of the building looks on to the Grand Canal, while the landward entrance is in Campiello del Remer, so called because there used to be an oarmaker's (remo means 'oar') workshop near by. It is one of the most charming, picturesque parts of Venice, and once there stood here a Gothic palazzo that belonged to the Lion family. All that survives today is the stunning external staircase with large arches that John Ruskin illustrated. The more modest Palazzo Remer, albeit from a later period, is built on Gothic lines. The piano nobile boasts an off-centre three-light window with a continuous balcony and a string course that marks off the ground floor from the two upper storeys. In an overall plan that makes a feature of its lack of symmetry, the canal entrance is the palazzo's only central element. In 1986 the architect Paolo Piva carried out far-reaching restoration work on the entire edifice, including the replacement of all the inside flooring. The work was done by the Asin company, which employed the ancient technique of Venetian mosaic, or terrazzo, but with modern decorative motifs designed by Piva.

56 PALAZZO ALBRIZZI
About 1600 and 1648–92
Vicenza sandstone paving flooring from 1986, to a design by Pia Nainer, Antonio Foscari and Ferruccio Franzoia, executed by Paolo Morseletto
San Polo (private: visitors not admitted)

Palazzo Albrizzi stands not far from Campo Sant'Aponal, in a somewhat peripheral position with respect to the Grand Canal. It was built in the sixteenth century for the Bonomo family, and purchased by the Albrizzis between 1648 and 1692. Until 1636, the area where the garden is today was occupied by San Cassiano, Europe's first public theatre. The architecture is uncompromising, and the interior of the palazzo still houses the most lavishly sumptuous stuccowork in Venice, especially on the mezzanine floor and ballroom, which have been attributed to Abbondio Stazio. The top floor of the building has a huge ship's-keel ceiling. It became a place for living or meditating, with a venerable collection of books (the Zenobio library). Thanks to apertures facing in the directions of the four cardinal points of the compass, the space offers memorable all-round perspectives of Venice and the lagoon. From this unique vantage-point, the glimpses of façades, domes, campanili (bell-towers) and roofs acquire an irresistible fascination.

57 PALAZZO LEZZE AT SANTO STEFANO
15th century
Trachyte paving from 1990 to a design by Antonio Foscari and Barbara Del Vicario, in collaboration with Ferruccio Franzoia, executed by Paolo Morseletto
San Marco (private: visitors not admitted)

Until the early eighteenth century, Campo Santo Stefano presented a gaily coloured scene, and the frescoes of Palazzo Lezze, like those of the two neighbouring houses, or so tradition had it, were the work of Giorgione. Today, however, this building, with its double entrance, and which originally had only two floors, is faced in brick. There are two great series of windows with seven ogival apertures on the façade, and those on the first floor are framed by a Greek marble surround. Recent restoration work has linked the entrance and the courtyard to the rear, where the wellhead is the central feature. Visual unity is achieved thanks to the wide opening and above all by the continuous longitudinal fascias in the paving of smooth trachyte, a material generally used out of doors. Light entering through the glazed partition enhances the typically Venetian materials, such as the wood of the beams and the original brick of the far wall.

58 HOTEL LUNA

18th century, restructured in 1992 by Carlo Aymonino and Gabriella Barbini
Floor in coloured marble from 1992, to a design by Gabriella Barbini, executed by the Menini company.
San Marco 1256

From as early as the ninth century, this was a lodging for pilgrims making their way to the East to fight the Mohammedan hordes who fought under the banner of the crescent moon. That was why it became known as the 'hostaria della luna', or 'tavern of the moon', a name it has kept down to the present day. Thought to be one of the most ancient lodging houses in Venice, the Hotel Luna was radically restructured in 1992 by Carlo Aymonino and Gabriella Barbini. The external façades have conserved their eighteenth-century design but were completely replastered by the *coccio pesto*, or 'crushed terracotta', technique. The marble floors in the hall and ground-floor reception rooms are especially noteworthy for their design, colour combinations and materials, which were inspired by the decorations of the city's churches and confraternities.

59 LABORATORIO ORSONI

19th century
Floor from 1996 by Lucio Orsoni
Cannaregio (private: visitors not admitted)

The Laboratorio Orsoni is situated in Calle dei Vedei, an area where the place names (Vedei means 'calves' in the Venetian dialect) and the adjacent public slaughterhouse remind us that it used to be pasture. The Laboratorio itself is part of a complex extending over about 1500 square metres and comprises three buildings arranged in a crown around the edges of a large open space closed off, on the side facing the calle, by a crenellated wall. The Laboratorio Orsoni dates from 1853, when it was built as a candlemaker's workshop. A few years later it was converted into a glass-bead factory, and then, in 1910, it became Angelo Orsoni's mosaic tesserae, workshop. Orsoni was the founder of a dynasty that still continues to produce tesserae, and the company's products are used every day all over the world. The internal configuration of the building has remained more or less unchanged since 1853. The tesserae are made in the premises on Rio del Battello, so called because a bridge could not be built on what is ecclesiastical property, with the result that a *battello*, or boat, was needed to cross the canal. The internal prospect features a series of pillars and cornices framing the doors and windows. The older building alongside was once used as a puppet theatre but today is the warehouse where the glass tiles and tesserae are stored, the interior of which is illuminated by their reflected light. The cutting and engraving workshop is in the most modern part of the complex, as are the administrative offices and the reception area, the floor of which offers an object lesson in the decorative potential offered by the modest squares of glass paste that the Laboratorio Orsoni continues so skilfully to produce.

GLOSSARY *by Antonio Crovato*

androne/**entrance hall** the entrance to a palazzo leading from the canal to the internal courtyard. The layout is repeated on the upper floors of the palazzo.

battuto a name for terrazzo, or Venetian mosaic, flooring in lime obtained by pounding the surface.

bindello a long, thin band (that may be repeated several times) outlining the decoration and separating the various background areas.

buccellato stone paving hammered into place by hand.

calce aerea/**common or air-hardening lime** a white solid obtained by baking limestone in special kilns.

carchedonie/**chalcedony** a natural variety of attractively coloured, translucent, fibrous or banded silica that was widely used in ancient times for jewellery.

campo/**background** the central portion of the floor when it is made up of one or more bands.

casin, casino "the name for certain small dwellings or rooms where a specific group of individuals meets to gamble or enjoy some other entertainment, especially during the night hours" *Tassini*.

ciottolo a roundish stone that is transformed into lime at about 800° C. If the process is incomplete, the stone has a crystalline appearance and is suitable for cutting. After crushing and screening, it acquires a pure white colour. Mixed with other granulated stones, it lends a particularly brilliant light to the terrazzo surface.

coccio pesto/**crushed terracotta** fragments of crushed terracotta and *ciottolo* lime.

commesso/**marble inlay** the flooring surface obtained by laying marble slabs of different shapes, sizes and colours flush with each other.

dodecahedron a regular polyhedron in which the twelve sides are regular convex pentagons.

fascia a relatively broad decorative border that normally runs round the perimeter of the terrazzo floor but may also frame the various geometrical figures that make up the pattern. Fascias may feature a vast range of ornamental motifs.

granello any of the minuscule rounded particles that may be found in marble lime, cement or powder.

intarsio/**inlay** the art of inserting pieces of stone or other material into specially prepared indentations in a surface.

lastrego paving.

liagò from the Greek *heliakon*: indicates a portion of the house exposed to the sun and used as a belvedere, or viewing-point. Over time, the two purposes became distinct. The small wooden construction built on the roof to enjoy the sun was called the *altana*, while the term *liagò* came to signify only the extension, usually in wood, added along an external wall, from which it was possible to look out without being seen.

litostròto a mosaic floor made from stones of different sizes, shapes and colours in very simple geometric patterns.

lucidare/**polishing** adding lustre to the surface of the terrazzo. The methods used include polishing with linseed oil and rags, wax, an *orso*, or 'bear', an implement comprising a block of sandstone attached to a long-handled iron support, with lime, with a 'lead' polishing machine, with special grinding machines or with oxalic acid

lucidare a piombo/**'lead' polishing** the kind of polishing that was once applied to cement floors. Special abrasives, to which small lead balls had been added, were used, or felts with iron rods. Today the method has been replaced by spongy, lacquer and oxalic acid-based abrasives.

masegno (pl. *masegni*) blocks of Euganean trachyte used for paving, often marked off by bands of Istrian stone. Laid either in line or edge to edge.

mosaico/**mosaic** an inlay of small pieces of various kinds of material (stone, marble, glass paste and so on) used to decorate floors and walls.

opus alexandrinum an interlacing mosaic floor pattern comprising marble tesserae in two different colours (for example, red and black or red and green) on a plain, usually white, background.

opus sectile a floor or wall cladding in different coloured slabs of marble cut into geometrical shapes, almost always rectangular, or sometimes to make other, non-geometrical patterns.

opus tessellatum mosaic made from small cubes of coloured marble.

opus vermiculatum walls or mosaics in which the blocks of stone or marble tesserae are arranged in irregular channels resembling worm tracks.

Palladiana/**Palladian** in the mosaicists' terminology, 'Palladian' refers to flooring with an irregular surface of marble chippings cut from 12–20-mm-thick slabs, arranged to leave as little space as possible between one piece and the next.

pasta/**paste** a special stucco made from a fine powder of marble and terracotta, lime and water.

pastellon flooring made from lime, fragments of terracotta brick and stone chippings, amalgamated thoroughly using a *becanela* (pile-driver), and covered with a thin layer of terracotta crushed and mixed with *ciottolo* lime. In ancient times, the mixture was coloured red with cinnabar.

pelta an elliptical decorative motif with one or two half-moon indentations in the upper part. The name comes from a kind of light shield used in Ancient Greece.

pòrtego the main reception room, which generally terminated in a portico on the ground floor and in a multiple-light window on the upper floors.

presbiterio/**presbytery** the part of a church around the high altar reserved for the clergy, often closed off by panels, screens, columns or pillars.

rappezzo a portion of terrazzo that has been relaid to incorporate earlier work. The mosaicist's skill lies in making the new elements as similar as possible to the existing flooring, like invisible mending.

ritaglio the fragments of marble produced when slabs or stones are cut, and from the working of marble in general. They are crushed to obtain a fine granular powder.

Sansovina a painted beam, characteristic of Venetian houses, so called because of the wide use made of them by the architect Jacopo Sansovino.

sagoma the practice of stretching strings between two points, or of using wooden or metal templates, especially in the nineteenth century, to obtain a precise, perfectly symmetrical design.

sagrato the open space in front of a church.

scaglia a generic name for granular marble chippings. *Scaglia grossa* is the name for pieces of cut marble for Palladian flooring.

semina granular chippings ready to be used for terrazzo flooring.

seminare/**'sowing'** careful distribution of the *semina* over the *stabilitura* bed.

sottofondo a layer of aggregates mixed with lime or cement laid on the floor. Laying terrazzo *di fondo*, means building it up completely from the lowest level to the surface.

stabilitura the application of the final layer of special mortar, made from granules of crushed marble with a diameter of about one centimetre, over which chippings will be scattered.

stuccatura/**stuccoing** the application to ancient floors of soft stucco with a palette knife. The surface is then sprinkled with chalk and left for a week, a sufficient interval before the subsequent stages of polishing with the hand-held *orso* ('bear') polisher and oiling.

stucco a compound of baked French chalk and oil used to stucco terrazzo floors.

tagliapietra/**stonemason** called *tajapiera* in Venetian; a stonecutter or squarer, a skilled worker in stone and marble.

terrazziere called *terrazer* in Venetian; someone skilled at laying terrazzo, or Venetian mosaic, floors.

terrazzo/**Venetian mosaic** the classic flooring surface for interiors, comprising pieces of marble in different shapes, colours and dimensions strewn over a bed of lime or cement mortar and abraded to a perfectly smooth finish. Also known in Italian as *pavimento alla veneziana*.

Corpus des mosaïques de Tunisie: *Utique*, I, no. 2, Tunis (Institut
National d'Archéologie et d'Art) 1974, nos. 146–242

Giorgione a Venezia, Milan (Electa) 1978

Isabella Reale, ed. 'Mosaico', Pordenone (Biblioteca dell'immagine)
1997

Leonardo e Venezia, Milan (Bompiani) 1992

Longhena, exhib. cat., Lugano, Villa Malpensata, 1982

Palazzo Mocenigo, sale cat., Venice, Christie's, 7–8 October 1996

Piazza San Marco. L'architettura, la storia, le funzioni, Venice
(Marsilio) 1970

Sols de l'Afrique romaine, Paris (Imprimerie Nationale) 1995

Testimonianze Palladiane, exhib. cat., Venice, Archivio di Stato di
Venezia, 28 June–28 September 1980

Venise au temps des galères, Paris (Hachette) 1968.

Ackerman, James S., *Palladio*, London (Penguin Books) 1966,
reprinted 1991

Alazraki, Paolo, and Maria Grazia Sandri, *Arte e vita ebraica a Venezia
1516–1797*, Florence (Sansoni) 1981

Alberti, Leon Battista, *L'Architettura. De re aedificatoria*, Milan
(Edizioni Polifilo) 1966

Albertini, Bianca, and Sandro Bagnoli, *Scarpa. L'architettura nel
dettaglio*, Milan (Jaca Book) 1988

Amendolagine, Francesco, Sergio Barizza, Roberto de Feo and Silvia
Moretti, *Palazzo Bonfadini-Vivante*, Venice (Arsenale Editrice) 1995

Bairati, Cesare, *La simmetria dinamica. Scienza ed arte
nell'architettura classica*, Milan (Politecnica Tamburini) 1952

Balty, Janine, *Mosaïque antiques de Syrie*, Brussels 1977

Barral y Altet, Xavier, *Les mosaïques de pavement medievales de Venise,
Murano, Torcello*, Paris (Picard) 1985

Basaldella, Francesco, *Giudecca. Cenni storici*, Venice 1983

Bassi, Elena, *Architettura del Sei e Settecento a Venezia*, Naples
(Edizioni scientifiche italiane) 1962

Bassi, Elena, *Il Convento della Carità*, Vicenza (Centro internazionale
di studi di architettura A. Palladio) 1971

Bassi, Elena, *Palazzi di Venezia. Admiranda urbis Venetae*, Venice (La
Stamperia di Venezia) 1976

Bassi, Elena, *Tracce di chiese veneziane distrutte. Ricostruzioni dai
disegni di Antonio Visentini. Memorie*, LXXI, Venice (Istituto
Veneto di Scienze, Lettere ed Arti) 1997

Bassi, Elena, Alessandro Franchini and Rodolfo Pallucchini, *Palazzo Loredan e l'Istituto Veneto di Scienze, Lettere ed Arti*, Venice (Istituto Veneto di Scienze, Lettere ed Arti) 1985

Beigbeder, Olivier, *Lexique des symboles*, Geneva 1969

Bellavitis, Giorgio, and Giandomenico Romanelli, *Venezia*, Rome and Bari (Laterza) 1985

Benoist, Luc, *Segni, simboli e miti*, trans. into Italian by Ada Beltramelli, Milan (Garzanti) 1976

Berti, Bruno (ed.), *La basilica di San Marco, arte e simbologia*, Venice (Studium Cattolico Veneziano) 1993

Bettini, Sergio, *L'architettura di San Marco*, Padua (Le Tre Venezie) 1946

Bettini, Sergio (ed.), *Venezia e Bisanzio*, exhib. cat., 8 June–30 September 1974, Venice (Alfieri) 1974

Boi, Ennio, *Il palazzo Soranzo Piovene, sede dell'ufficio del generale di divisione ispettore della Guardia di Finanza per l'Italia nord orientale*, Venice 1995

Boucher, Bruce, *Andrea Palladio: The Architect in His Time*, New York (Abbeville) 1994

Branca, Vittore (ed.), *Barocco europeo e barocco veneziano*, Florence (Sansoni) 1962

Bruyère, André, *Sols. Saint-Marc Venise*, Paris (Imprimerie Nationale) 1990

Calimani, Riccardo, *Storia del ghetto di Venezia*, Milan (Rusconi) 1985

Caniato, Giovanni, and Michaela dal Borgo, *Le arti edili a Venezia*, Rome (Edil Stampa) 1990

Carlevarijs, Luca, *Le fabbriche e vedute di Venezia, disegnate, poste in prospettiva e intagliate, con priviligii*, Venice 1703

Chevalier, Jean, and Alain Gheerbrant, *Dictionnaire des symboles*, Paris (R. Laffont) 1969

Chiappini di Sorio, Ileana, *Palazzo Pisani Moretta*, Milan (Franco Maria Ricci) 1983

Cicogna, Pasquale, *Iscrizioni veneziane*, MS 2022, Venice (Biblioteca Museo Correr)

Concina, Ennio, *Storia dell'architettura di Venezia dal VII al XX secolo*, Milan (Electa) 1995

Conty, Patrick, *Labirinti*, Casale Monferrato (TO), (Piemme) 1997

Cooperman, Bernard D., and Roberta Curiel, *Il ghetto di Venezia*, Venice (Arsenale Editrice) 1990

Corner, Flaminio, *Notizie storiche delle chiese e monasteri di Venezia e di Torcello*, Padua (Stamperia del Seminario G. Manfrè) 1758

Coryat, Thomas, *Crudezze. Viaggio in Francia e in Italia* 1608, ed. Franco Marengo and Antonio Meo, Milan (Longanesi) 1975

Crovato, Antonio, *I pavimenti alla veneziana*, Venice (L'Altra Riva) 1989

Cunaccia, Cesare M., and Mark E. Smith, *Interni a Venezia*, Venice (Arsenale Editrice) 1994

Cuschito, Giuseppe, *Grado e le sue basiliche paleocristiane*, Bologna (Fotocrome Emiliana) 1992

Da Mosto, Andrea, *I dogi di Venezia nella vita pubblica e privata*, Milan (Martello) 1966

Damerini, Gino, *Settecento veneziano. La vita, gli amori, i nemici di Caterina Dolfin Tron*, Milan 1939

Damerini, Gino, *D'Annunzio e Venezia*, Verona (Mondadori) 1943

Damerini, Gino, *L'isola e il cenobio di San Giorgio Maggiore*, Venice (Fondazione Cini) 1969

Daszeswski, W.A., and D. Michaelides, *Guide to the Paphos Mosaics*, Nicosia (Bank of Cyprus) 1988

Davanzo Poli, Doretta, and Stefania Moronato, *Il Museo di Palazzo Mocenigo*, Milan (Electa) 1995

De Min, Maurizia, 'Venezia. Rinvenimenti medievali nella chiesa di San Lorenzo. Notizie preliminari', *Venezia Arti*, 4, 1990

De Vecchi, Pierluigi, *Tintoretto*, Milan (Rizzoli) 1970

Di Nola, Alfonso, *Cabbala e mistica giudaica*, Rome (Carucci) 1984

Dorigato, Attilia, and Giuseppe Mazzariol, *Interni veneziani*, Padua, (Biblos) 1989

Dorigo, Wladimiro, *Venezia. Origini*, Milan (Electa) 1983

Fabbiani, Licia, *La fondazione monastica di San Nicolò di Lido (1053–1628)*, Venice (Ufficio affari istituzionali del Comune di Venezia) n.d.

Falchetta, Piero, 'La misura dipinta. Rilettura tecnica e semantica della veduta di Venezia di Jacopo de' Barbari', in *Ateneo Veneto*, Venice 1991

Farioli Campanati, Raffaella, 'Il pavimento di San Marco a Venezia e i suoi rapporti con l'Oriente', in Renato Polacco (ed.), *Storia dell'arte marciana. I mosaici*, Venice (Marsilio) 1997

Figelli, Nicoletta, *Guida di Aquileia*, Trieste (Fachin) 1991

Fiorini, Guido, *Saggio su tracciati armonici*, Rome (Tipografia della Pace) 1958

Florent-Goudoneix, Ivette, 'Il pavimento della Basilica', in *Basilica Patriarcale in Venezia, i mosaici, le iscrizioni, la Pala d'Oro*, Milan (Fabbri Bompiani Sanzogno) 1991

Florent-Goudoneix, Ivette, 'I pavimenti in "opus sectile" nelle chiese di Venezia', in Renato Polacco (ed.), *Storia dell'arte marciana. I mosaici*, Venice (Marsilio) 1997

Fontana, Gian Jacopo, *I principali palazzi di Venezia*, Venice (Scarbelli) 1865

Forlati, Ferdinando, *La basilica di San Marco attraverso i suoi restauri*, Trieste (Edizioni Lint) 1975

Foscari, Antonio, and Barbara del Vicario, *Relazione storica di Palazzo Contarini Cavalli*, Venice 1983

Foscari, Lodovico, *Affreschi esterni a Venezia*, Milan (Stucchi) 1936

Fradier, Georges, *Mosaïques romaines de Tunisie*, Tunis (Cérès) 1986

Gemin, Massimo, and Filippo Pedrocco, *Giambattista Tiepolo. I dipinti. Opera completa*, Venice (Arsenale Editrice) 1993

Ghyka, Matila C., *Esthétique des proportions dans la nature et dans les arts*, Paris (Gallimard) 1927

Ghyka, Matila C., *Le nombre d'or*, I: *Les rythmes*; II: *Les rites*, Paris, (Gallimard) 1931

Ghyka, Matila C., *Essay sur le rythme*, Paris (Gallimard) 1938

Gianighian, Giorgio, and Paola Pavanini (eds.), *Dietro i palazzi. Tre secoli di architettura minore a Venezia (1492–1803)*, Venice (Arsenale Editrice) 1984

Gramigna, Silvia, and Annalisa Perissa, *Scuole di arti, mestieri e devozione a Venezia*, Venice (Arsenale Editrice) 1981

Iacumin, Renato, *La basilica di Aquileia. Il mosaico dell'aula nord*, Reana del Rojale (UD) (Chiandetti) 1990

Ivanoff, Nicola, *Venezia San Giorgio Maggiore, tesori d'arte cristiana*, no. 74, 29 July 1967

James, Henry, *The Wings of the Dove* [1902], London (Penguin Books) 1986

Jacopo, Bellini, *L'album dei disegni del Louvre*, Milan (Jaca Book) 1984

Kerényi, Karoly, *Nel labirinto*, Turin (Bollati Boringheri) 1983

Krauss, Rosalind, *Grids*, New York (MIT Press) 1994

Lane, Frederic C., *Storia di Venezia*, Turin (Einaudi) 1978

Lauritzen, Peter, *Palaces of Venice*, Florence (Beocci) 1978

Links, J.G., *Venice for Pleasure*, London (The Bodley Head) 1966

Longhi, Roberto, *Viatico per cinque secoli di pittura veneziana*, Florence (Sansoni) 1952

Lorenzetti, Giulio, *Itinerario sansoviniano a Venezia*, ed. Comitato per le onoranze sansoviniane, Venice 1929

Lorenzetti, Giulio, *Venezia e il suo estuario. Guida storico-artistica*, Rome (Istituto poligrafico dello Stato, Libreria dello Stato) 1956

Magagnato, Licisco (ed.), *Le stoffe di Cangrande. Ritrovamenti e ricerche sul Trecento veronese*, Florence (Alinari) 1983

Marcuzzi, Luigi, *Aquileia*, Sacile (PN) (Zanetti) 1985

Maretto, Paolo, *Venezia*, Genoa (Vitali e Ghianda) 1969

Maretto, Paolo, *L'edilizia gotica veneziana*, Venice (Filippi) 1978

Maretto, Paolo, *La casa veneziana nella storia della città dalle origini all'Ottocento*, Venice (Marsilio) 1986

Mariacher, Giovanni, *Tempio del Santissimo Redentore. Venezia*, Bologna (Poligrafici Il Resto del Carlino) 1967

Mazzariol, Giuseppe, and Giuseppe Barbieri, *Carlo Scarpa 1906–1978*, Milan (Electa) 1984

Mazzucco, Gabriele (ed.), *Monasteri benedettini nella laguna veneziana*, Venice (Arsenale Editrice) 1983

McAndrew, John, *Venetian Architecture of the Early Renaissance*, Cambridge MA and London (MIT Press) 1980

McCarthy, Mary, *Venice Observed*, New York (Harvest Book, Harcout, Brace & World) 1963

Mistrorigo, Teresa, *L'abbazia di Pomposa*, Bologna (La Fotocromo Emiliana) 1971

Moldi Ravenna, Cristiana, Tudy Sammartini and Gianni Berengo Gardin, *Giardini segreti a Venezia*, Venice (Arsenale Editrice) 1988

Molmenti, Pompeo, *La storia di Venezia nella vita privata dalle origini alla caduta della Repubblica*, 3 vols., Bergamo (Istituto italiano d'arti graficheo) 1922–27

Montaigne, Michel de, *Viaggio in Italia (1580–1581)*, trans. into Italian by Irene Riboli, Milan (Bompiani) 1942

Morris, Jan, *The Venetian Empire*: *A Sea Voyage*, London and Boston (Faber and Faber) 1980

Morris, James, *Venice*, London (Faber and Faber) 1960

Moschini, Giannantonio, *Itinéraire de Venise*, Venice 1818

Moschini, Giannantonio, *Ragguaglio delle cose notabili nella chiesa e nel seminario patriarcale di Santa Maria della Salute in Venezia*, Venice (Tipografia di Alvisopoli) 1819

Moschini Marconi, Sandra, *Galleria G. Franchetti alla Ca' D'Oro*, Rome (Istituto Poligrafico e Zecca dello Stato) 1992

Moschini Marconi, Sandra, *Gallerie dell'Accademia di Venezia. Opere d'arte dei secoli XIV e XV*, Rome (Istituto Poligrafico dello Stato) 1955

Muraro, Michelangelo, *Palazzo Contarini a San Beneto*, Venice (Stamperia di Venezia) 1970

Muraro, Michelangelo, and André Grabar, *Les trésor de Venise*, Geneva (Skira) 1963

Norwich, John Julius, *Venice*, 2 vols., I: *The Rise to Empire*, London (Allen Lane) 1977; II: *The Greatness and the Fall*, London (Allen Lane) 1981; republished in one volume as *A History of Venice*, London (Allen Lane) 1982, reprinted London (Penguin Books) 1983

Pacioli, Luca, *De divina proportione*, ed. Associazione fra le Casse di Risparmio Italiane di Roma, Milan (Silvana Editoriale) 1982

Palladio, Andrea, *I quattro libri dell'architettura*, Venice (Domenico de' Franceschi) 1570

Pallucchini, Anna, *Giambattista Tiepolo*, Milan (Rizzoli) 1968

Paoletti, Ermolao, *Il fiore di Venezia*, Venice (Tipografia Fontana) 1839

Paoletti, Pietro, *L'architettura e la scultura del Rinascimento in Venezia*, Venice 1893

Paoletti, Pietro, 'La Ca' d'Oro', in *Studio di Arte e Storia*, ed. Museo Civico Correr, vol. I, Milan and Rome 1920

Pasini, Antoine, *Guide à la Basilique de S. Marc à Venise*, Schio (VI) (L. Marin) 1888

Pavanello, Giuseppe, and Giandomenico Romanelli (eds.), *Venezia nell'Ottocento. Immagini e mito*, exhib. cat., Milano (Electa) 1983

Perosa, Sergio (ed.), *Henry James e Venezia*, Florence (Olsky) 1987

Perry, Marilyn, *The Basilica of SS. Maria e Donato on Murano*, Venice (Stamperia di Venezia) 1980

Pertusi, Agostino (ed.), *Venezia e l'Oriente fra tardo Medioevo e Rinascimento*, Florence (Sansoni) 1966

Pignatti, Teresio, *Il quaderno dei disegni del Canaletto*, Milan (Daria Guarnati) 1958

Polacco, Renato, *La cattedrale di Torcello*, Venice (L'Altra Riva) and Treviso (Canova) 1984

Polacco, Renato, 'Il pavimentum sectile di San Marco', *Venezia Arti*, no. 4, 1990

Popescu, Grigore Arbore, and Sergio Zoppi, *Palazzo Papadopoli a Venezia*, Venice (Consiglio Nazionale delle Ricerche) 1993

Proust, Marcel, *La fuggitiva*, Milan (Rizzoli) 1991

Puppi, Lionello, *L'opera completa di Canaletto*, Milan (Rizzoli) 1968

Puppi, Lionello (ed.), *Palladio a Venezia*, Florence (Sansoni) 1982

Puppi, Lionello, 'Venezia come Gerusalemme nella cultura figurativa del Rinascimento', in August Buck and Bodo Guthmiller (eds.), *La città italiana del Rinascimento fra utopia e realtà*, Quaderno del Centro tedesco di studi veneziani, no. 27, Venice 1984

Puppi, Lionello, and Giandomenico Romanelli (eds.), *Le Venezie possibili. Da Palladio a Le Corbusier*, exhib. cat., Milan (Electa) 1985

Quadri, Antonio, *Huit jours à Venise*, Venice (A. Bazzarini) 1838

Quadri, Antonio, *Il Canal Grande di Venezia*, Venice 1886

Ragghianti, Carlo L., 'La crosera de Piazza di Carlo Scarpa', *Zodiac*, IV, 1 April 1959

Reato, Danilo, *Il caffè Florian*, Venice (Filippi) 1984

Reato, Danilo, and Elisabetta Dal Carlo, *La bottega del caffè. I caffè veneziani tra '700 e '900*, Venice (Arsenale Editrice) 1991

Reinisch Sullam, Giovannina, *Il ghetto di Venezia, le sinagoghe e il museo*, Rome (Carucci) 1985

Ridolfi, Carlo, *Le meraviglie dell'arte ovvero le vite degli illustri pittori Veneti e dello Stato*, ed. Detlev von Hadeln, 2 vols., Berlin 1914–21

Ripa, Cesare, *Iconologia* [Rome 1593], 2 vols., Turin (Fogola) 1986

Rizzi, Aldo, *Luca Carlevarijs*, Venice (Alfieri) 1967

Romanelli, Giandomenico, *Venezia Ottocento. Materiali per una storia architettonica e urbanistica della città nel secolo XIX*, Rome (Officina) 1977

Romanelli, Giandomenico, *Tra Gotico e Neogotico*, Venice (Albrizzi) 1990

Romanelli, Giandomenico, and Mark E. Smith, *Ritratto di Venezia*, Venice (Arsenale Editrice) 1996

Romano, Ruggero, and Angelo Schwarz, *Per una storia della farmacia e del farmacista in Italia. Venezia e Veneto*, Bologna (Skema) 1981

Ruskin, John, *The Stones of Venice*, ed. Jan Morris, Boston and Toronto (Little, Brown) 1981

Sabellico, Marc'Antonio, *Del sito di Venezia città* [1502], ed. G. Meneghetti, Venice (Stamperia già Zanetti) 1957

Salerni, Lina, *Repertorio delle opere d'arte e dell'arredo delle chiese e delle scuole di Venezia*, vol. 1: *Dorsoduro–Giudecca–Santa Croce*, Vicenza (Neri Pozza) 1994

Sansoni, Umberto, *'Il Nodo di Salomone'*, Milan (Electa) 1998

Sansovino, Francesco, *Venetia città nobilissima et singolare con le aggiunte di Giustiniano Martinoni*, Venice (Stefano Curti) 1663

Santarcangeli, Paolo, *Il libro dei labirinti*, Milan (Frassinelli) 1984

Sanudo, Marin (il Giovane), *De origine, situ et magistratibus urbis Venetae, ovvero La città di Venezia (1493–1530)*, ed. Angela Caracciolo Aricò, Milan (Istituto editoriale cisalpino-goliardica) 1980

Scattolin, Francesca, 'I pavimenti scomparsi della Scuola Grande della Misericordia', *Venezia Arti*, 7, 1993

Scattolin, Giorgia, *Le case-fondaco sul Canal Grande*, Venice 1961

Schneider, Marius, *Gli animali simbolici e la loro origine musicale nella mitologia e nella scultura antiche*, Milan (Rusconi) 1986

Scoto, Francesco, *Itinerario ovvero nova descrittione di viaggi principali d'Italia di Francesco Scoto aggiontavi in quest'ultima impressione le descrittioni di Udine …*, Venice (Gio' Pietro Brigonci) 1665

Selincourt, Beryl de, and May Stinge Henderson, *Venice*, New York (Dodd, Mead) 1907

Selvatico, Pietro, *Sulla architettura e sulla scultura in Venezia dal Medioevo sino ai nostri giorni. Studi di P. Selvatico per servire di guida estetica*, Venice (P. Ripamonti Carpano) 1847

Shaw-Kennedy, Ronald, *Venice Rediscovered*, Philadelphia (Art Alliance Press) 1978

Smith Cristina, *Ravenne. L'age d'or*, Florence (Scala) 1977

Steinsaltz, Adin, *La rose aux treize pétales*: *Introduction à la Cabbale suivi de introduction au Talmud*, Paris (Albin Michel) 1996

Succi, Sandro (ed.), *Da Carlevarijs a Tiepolo. Incisori veneti e friulani del Settecento*, Venice (Albrizzi) 1983

Tafuri, Manfredo, *Venezia e il Rinascimento. Religione, scienza, architettura*, Turin (Einaudi) 1985

Tassini, Giuseppe, *Curiosità veneziane, ovvero origini delle denominazioni stradali*, ed. Lino Moretti, Venice (Filippi) 1964

Tassini, Giuseppe, *Edifici di Venezia distrutti o volti ad altro uso da quello a cui furono in origine destinati*, Venice (Filippi) 1969

Temanza, Tomaso, *Vite di più celebri architetti e scultori veneziani che fiorirono nel secolo decimosesto*, Venice (Stamperia C. Polese) 1778

Temanza, Tomaso, *Zibaldone (1738–1778)*, ed. Nicola Ivanoff, Venice and Rome (Istituto per la Collaborazione Culturale) 1963

Tongiorgi Tommasi, Lucia, *L'opera completa di Paolo Uccello*, Milan (Rizzoli) 1971

Tortorella, Stefano, 'Pavimentazioni a mosaico nel mondo romano', *I quaderni dell'Emilceramica*, 21, Faenza (Faenza Editrice) 1994

Trincanato Egle, Renata, *Venezia minore*, Venice (Filippi) 1948

Valcanover, Francesco, *Ca' d'Oro. La Galleria Giorgio Franchetti*, Milan (Electa) 1986

Varazze, Jacopo da, *Legenda Aurea (1228–1298)*, ed. Alessandro and Lucietta Vitale Barrerosa, Turin (Einaudi) 1995

Vasari, Giorgio, *Le vite de' più eccellenti pittori, scultori e architetti*, 7 vols., Florence (A. Salani) 1927–32

Vaudoyer, Jean-Louis, *Les délices de l'Italie*, Paris (Plon-Nourrit) 1924

Vitoux, Frédéric, *L'Arte di vivere a Venezia*, Milan (Mondadori) n.d.

Whittick, Arnold (ed.), *Ruskin's Venice*, London (George Godwin) 1976

Wilson, Edward D., 'The Right Place', in *Biophilia*, Cambridge MA (Harvard University Press) 1984

Zanetti Anton Maria, *Varie pitture a fresco de' principali maestri veneziani*, Venice 1760

Zanetti, Anton Maria, *Della pittura veneziana e delle opere pubbliche dei veneziani maestri*, Venice (G. Storti) 1792

Zanetti, Anton Maria, *Descrizione di tutte le pubbliche pitture della città di Venezia ed isole circonvicine* [Venice, P. Basaglia, 1733], Bologna (A. Forni) 1980

Zanotto, Francesco, *Nuovissima guida di Venezia e delle isole della sua laguna*, Venice (G. Brizeghel) 1865

Zorzi, Alvise, *La Repubblica del Leone*, Milan (Rusconi) 1979

Zorzi, Alvise, *Venezia scomparsa*, Milan (Electa) 1984

Zorzi, Marino, *La Libreria di San Marco*, Milan (Arnoldo Mondadori, 1987

Zucchetta, Emmanuela, *Antichi ridotti veneziani*, Rome (Palombi) 1988

Zucconi, Guido, *Venezia Guida all'architettura*, Venice (Arsenale Editrice) 1993

ACKNOWLEDGEMENTS *by Tudy Sammartini*

I should like to thank Elena Bassi, whose books *Architettura del Sei e Settecento a Venezia* and *Palazzi di Venezia* have provided me with much useful information, and without which I would never have been able to tackle this work. I thank Cinzia Boscolo for checking and correcting my manuscript, Giulia Calligaro for polishing my introductory text, and Antonio Crovato for the technical information.

Thanks for their invaluable help is owed to: Feliciano Benvenuti, Bruno Bertoli, Anna Maria Cadel, Lulli Chiappini, Doretta Davanzo Poli, Barbara Del Vicario, Gianni Fabbri, Daulo Foscolo, Silvia Lunardon, Marina Magrini, Lesa Marcello, Antonio Niero, Luigi Savio, Francesca Scattolin, Rossana Serandrei Barbero, Piergiogio Tempesti and Lina Urban.

I am grateful to the city institutions that allowed me access to their buildings: Associazone Alliance Française (Antonio Foscari, President; Frédéric Bouilleux, French Embassy Cultural Attaché); Azienda Multiservizi Ambientali Veneziana (Guido Berro, President; Antonio Stifanelli, Director General; Daniela Mattarucco); Banca Commerciale Italiana (central management in Milan and of the San Marco branch in Venice); Biblioteca Nazionale Marciana (Marino Zorzi, Director; Piero Falchetta); Consiglio Internazionale delle Ricerche (Grigore Arbore Popescu, Researcher); Compagnia Generale delle Acque (Paolo Salvaduz, Administrative Director); Communità Ebraica (Giovannina Reinisch Sullam); Corte d'Appello, ufficio di Presidenza; Curia Patriarcale (Don Matteo Caputo, Director of the Cultural Heritage Office, and the parish priests of various churches); Direzione Civici Musei Veneziani (Giandomenico Romanelli, Director; Stafania Moronato, Curator of the Palazzo Mocenigo; Flavia Scotton, Curator of the Galleria d'Arte Moderna); Fondazione Scientifica Querini Stampalia (Giorgio Busetto, Director; Mariagusta Lazzari; Angelo Mini); Guardia di Finanzia (Lorenzo Reali, Divisional Dirctor and Inspector for north-east Italy); Istituto Veneto di Scienza, Lettere ed Arti (Alessandro Franchini, Director); Mediovenezie Banca SpA; Orsoni Angelo snc; Procuratoria di San Marco (Monsignor Antonio Meneguolo, Secretary; Ettore Vio, Registrar; Maria Da Villa Urbani; Andrea Bianchini); Soprintendenza ai beni ambientali e architettonici di Venezia (Maurizia De Min; Emanuela Zucchetta; Maria Trevenzoli; Stefano Seragiò); Soprintendenza ai beni artistici e storici di Venezia (Giovanna Nepi Scirè, Superintendent; Adriana Ruggeri Augusti; Sandra Moschini Marconi; Antonio Martini); Scuola Grande dei Carmini (Lamberto della Tofola Guardian Grando; Vanda Miori).

Finally, for their kind help and availability, I should like to thank: Giovanni Allata di Montereale, the Armenian fathers, Bianca Arrivabene Gonzaga, Paolo and Donatella Asta, Stefano Baccara, Gabriella Barbini, Gianfranco Baroncelli, Brando Brandolini d'Adda, Maria Camerino, Maurizio d'Este, Mariolina Doria de Zuliani, Alberto Falck, Francesca Forni, Caterina Fuga, Achille and Grazia Gaggia, Maria Franchin Donà dalle Rose, Peter and Rosy Lauritzen, Luciano Luciani, Lucio Orsoni, Francesco and Mario Pasetti-Bombardella, Paolo Piva, Rino Rizzo, Adriana Rocca, Ernesto Rubin de Cervin Albrizzi, Natale Rusconi, Edoardo Salzano, Maurizio and Barbara Sammartini, Leonardo Tiveran, Gianfranca Totti, Paolo Trentinaglia, Francesco Trevisanto, Romano and Daniela Vedaldi, Patricia Viganò Curtis, Loris Volpato, Paolo Volpe, Erica Zecca, Alessandro Zoppi, the directors of the hotels Bauer Grünwald, Cipriani, Europa & Regina, Luna and the ITT Sheraton Corporation.

A NOTE ON THE PHOTOGRAPHS *by Gabriele Crozzoli*

PICTURE CREDITS

This amazing journey across the decorative floors of Venice was conceived in the home of Elisabetta Czamocki, a dear friend who has drawn me closer to the spirit and essence of Venice and its illustrious history.

Photographing the decorative floors has been a major task that has lasted several years and presented quite a number of problems. Venice is beautiful, and quite unlike anywhere else in the world, but its interiors are not easy to photograph: technical solutions, particularly involving lighting, are needed in order to convey the unique patina of the past and render the subject as palpable as possible to the viewer. But Tudy, Michela, Livio and I have had faith in this project from the very beginning and have worked hard to bring it to fruition.

Now, when I look at these photographs, the smells and the age-old atmosphere of these stunning buildings come back to me: the fascination I experienced when photographing their exquisite floors was sometimes enough to make my head spin.

A fresh light cast on to the past as well as the present of Venice; a stroll across the city's ancient mosaics, as well as the floors of its modern institutions: this is what these photographs are about.

Sovraintendenza ai beni ambientali architettonici di Venezia	14, 15
Archivio fotografico Osvaldo Böhm	18, 20, 21
Archivio fotografico Museo Correr	23
Mark E. Smith	47
Daniele Resini	132
Dida Biggi	171

Fotolito Zincografia Verona

INDEX TO BUILDINGS

Page references in italic are to the photographs.
Page references in roman are to the Historical Notes.